Blowing the Whistle on Genocide

Shofar Supplements in Jewish Studies

Blowing the Whistle on Genocide

Josiah E. DuBois, Jr., and the Struggle for a U.S. Response to the Holocaust

Rafael Medoff

Purdue University Press / West Lafayette, Indiana

The cover to Arthur Morse's 1968 book, *While Six Million Died: A Chronicle of American Apathy,* showed President Franklin D. Roosevelt averting his eyes. This memorable illustration was the creation of renowned caricaturist Gerry Gersten. Over the years, he has drawn hundreds of book covers as well as illustrations for such publications as the *New York Times, Sports Illustrated,* and *Rolling Stone,* but this was the first time he had taken on a topic related to the Holocaust.

While Six Million Died* was the first book about America's response to the Holocaust. It was also the first book to identify Josiah E. DuBois, Jr., as one of the key figures pushing for a change in U.S. refugee policy. It is therefore particularly appropriate that Mr. Gersten has returned to the genre, for the first time in forty years, with his remarkable portrait of DuBois for the cover of *Blowing the Whistle on Genocide.*

Blowing the Whistle on Genocide

*Josiah E. DuBois, Jr. and the Struggle
for a U.S. Response to the Holocaust*

by Rafael Medoff
Foreword by Ambassador Stuart E. Eizenstat

Printed in the United States of America.

Library of Congress Cataloging-in-Publication Data

Medoff, Rafael, 1959–

  Blowing the whistle on genocide : Josiah E. DuBois, Jr. and the struggle for a U.S. response to the Holocaust / by Rafael Medoff

    p. cm. — (Shofar supplements in Jewish studies)

  Includes bibliographical references.

  ISBN 978-1-55753-507-8

  1. World War, 1939–1945—Jews—Rescue—United States. 2. Refugees, Jewish—Government policy—United States—History—20th century. 3. DuBois, Josiah E. (Josiah Ellis), 1912–1983. 4. United States. War Refugee Board. 5. United States—Foreign relations—1933–1945. 6. Roosevelt, Franklin D. (Franklin Delano), 1882–1945—Relations with Jews. 7. United States—Emigration and immigration—Government policy. 8. Holocaust, Jewish (1939–1945)—Influence. 9. United States—Ethnic relations. I. Wyman, David S. II. Title.

  D804.6.M43 2008

  940.53'1850973—dc22   2008012606

Contents

Acknowledgments

This book describes what Josiah E. DuBois, Jr., did to help bring about the rescue of Jews from the Holocaust. It is neither a biography of DuBois nor a comprehensive history of the War Refugee Board, the U.S. government rescue agency that he helped bring into existence and of which he was a leader. Those are books that remain to be written. DuBois's own memoir, *The Devil's Chemists*, mentioned only briefly and in passing what he did during the Holocaust.[1] He wrote almost exclusively about his postwar experiences as a prosecutor at the Nuremberg Trials. That period of his life is not part of the story on which I focus. In these pages, I seek to tell the story of his role in Holocaust rescue, through his own words and the words of those with whom he worked in this struggle. They are derived from previously unpublished interviews as well as documents from the period. Martin Ostrow, Lawrence Jarvik, Henry Morgenthau III, Lawrence Glaser, Richard Breitman, and Alan Kraut kindly made their interviews with the principal figures in this story available for my use, and I am grateful to them for doing so. Thanks, too, to Benyamin Korn, Prof. Harry Reicher, and David Lee Preston for their roles in the 2006 conference on DuBois, organized by The David S. Wyman Institute for Holocaust Studies and held at the University of Pennsylvania School of Law, DuBois's alma mater.

I acknowledge, with deepest appreciation, the generous support of the Lucius N. Littauer Foundation for publication of this book. I am likewise grateful for the assistance of the Josiah E. DuBois, Jr., Memorial Publication Committee, whose members, Richard Goodwin, Regine and Edward Barshak, Annette Lidawer, Bernice Zoslaw, Dr. Nathan Moskowitz, James Blum, and Dr. Jay Rothschild, facilitated the completion of this book. I am thankful to Prof. Richard Libowitz and Prof. Zev Garber for their many helpful comments on earlier versions of the manuscript, and to Professors Deborah Dwork, Alan Berger, David Dalin, and Leonard Swidler for their assistance and encouragement. I am also grateful to Gerry Gersten, for his extraordinary cover illustration, and Neal Adams, of Continuity Graphics, for assisting with the color scheme for the cover; to Dr. Nathan Moskowitz for his many helpful suggestions with regard to the artwork for this book; to Betty Igdalski Lawler, Esq., for her research assistance; and to Hank Sheinkopf and Austin Shafran of Sheinkopf, Ltd., for their help in bringing this book to greater public attention. And a special thanks to Purdue University Press director Thomas Bacher, author liaison Becki Corbin, production and design manager Bryan Shaffer, and copyeditor John Joerschke for making the publication of this book possible. Thanks, too, to Robert C. DuBois and his family for allowing reproduction of photographs of his father and mother.

This book is dedicated to my wife, Carin—as our sages teach, "He who finds a righteous wife, has found goodness and will find favor from the Lord" (Proverbs 18:22).

Note

1.   Josiah E. DuBois, Jr., *The Devil's Chemists* (Boston: The Beacon Press, 1952), 184–189, 197–199.

Foreword

By Ambassador Stuart E. Eizenstat[1]

American heroes come in different varieties—soldiers who distinguish themselves on the battlefield, political leaders who inspire a nation, sports figures who lift us up from our everyday lives with their athletic accomplishments. In his excellent book, *Blowing the Whistle on Genocide: Josiah E. DuBois, Jr., and the Struggle for a U.S. Response to the Holocaust*, Rafael Medoff makes it clear that Mr. DuBois, a little-known civil servant in the Treasury Department during World War II, was an American hero. He courageously exposed the failure of American policy to help victims of the Holocaust and catalyzed belated action by the Roosevelt administration to save European Jews from Hitler's hands.

During World War II, DuBois worked in the United States Treasury Department under Secretary Henry Morgenthau, Jr. As this book chronicles, it was DuBois who blew the whistle on the State Department's suppression of information about the massacres and its foot-dragging and blocking of plans that would have rescued Jews fleeing certain death.

When Morgenthau learned of this suppression from DuBois, it must have seemed sadly familiar. His father, Henry Morgenthau, Sr., had been President Woodrow Wilson's ambassador to the Ottoman Empire at the time of the mass slaughter of Armenians by the Ottoman Turks during World War I and had brought it to the attention of President Wilson and the American public. This book describes the fascinating twists and turns along the path that led from DuBois's discoveries to Morgenthau and ultimately to the White House. Thanks to the valiant efforts of DuBois and his colleagues, the United States finally acted in the waning months of the war to rescue Jews.

It is said in the Talmud that he who saves an individual life is as if he saved the entire world. This wisdom applies multiple times to Josiah DuBois. He saw wrong and worked to rectify it, even at the risk of his career.

My own path to serving as President Bill Clinton's special representative on Holocaust-era issues and bringing belated justice to more than one million Holocaust survivors and other victims of Nazi atrocities sixty years after World War II—through agreements with the Swiss, Germans, Austrians, French, and other European nations providing over $8 billion to survivors (most of it going to non-Jewish forced laborers)—began with a personal experience I had when I was research director for Vice President Hubert Humphrey's presidential campaign in 1968. One of my fellow campaign workers was Arthur Morse, a veteran investigative reporter and producer for CBS-TV. He had just authored an extraordinary book called *While Six Million Died: A Chronicle of American Apathy*. It was the first book to expose the failure of the Roosevelt administration to rescue European Jews from Hitler's clutches.

Morse discussed with me the book and his findings. It came as a great shock to me. Like most Americans of my generation, I grew up assuming that just as the U.S. government had led the successful military effort against Nazi Germany and Japan, so too, our government, and certainly President Franklin D. Roosevelt, had done everything possible to help Europe's Jews escape the Holocaust. Arthur Morse convinced me this had not been the case.

FDR had been an icon in my house and in the American Jewish community in general. President Roosevelt had been so venerated in the Jewish community that there was a Yiddish joke that Jews believed in three worlds (*velts*): "*die velt* (this world), *yenna velt* (the next world), and Roosevelt!" It was profoundly troubling to learn that the president and his inner circle of advisers, several of whom were Jewish, knew about the mass murder of the Jews and did so little to stop it.

After the war ended, there were several inadequate efforts at providing restitution and compensation for Holocaust survivors and other victims of Nazism, both Jews and non-Jews alike, from neutral countries. With the advent of the Cold War, all of America's efforts were turned to facing the new Soviet menace, and justice for those the U.S. government had done so little to save during the war took a back seat. It appeared that the fate of these survivors and their families would evaporate into the mists of history.

As the Clinton administration's leader in putting the issue of justice for the civilian victims of World War II back on the world agenda from my positions as U.S. ambassador to the European Union, under secretary of commerce, under secretary of state, and finally deputy secretary of the treasury, it was a source of inspiration to me personally to learn that my predecessors at the Treasury Department, Josiah DuBois and his colleagues, had tried to do the same six decades before and were unsung heroes whose courage helped change the course of history.

There is, in fact, a direct link from my encounter with Arthur Morse and his book in 1968 to the story of Josiah DuBois, the focal point of this book. It was Morse's book that first revealed the role of DuBois in convincing a reluctant Roosevelt administration to intervene against the Nazi slaughter. Now, in *Blowing the Whistle on Genocide*, Rafael Medoff finishes the job that Arthur Morse began, by telling for the first time the complete story of what DuBois did and what motivated him to take such heroic and selfless action. It is long overdue, and it is a story in which every American can take pride. We owe a debt of gratitude to Dr.

Medoff but an even bigger one to Josiah E. DuBois, Jr., who exemplified the noble spirit of public service and humanitarianism to which each of us should aspire.

Note

1. Stuart E. Eizenstat served as chief domestic policy adviser in the White House to President Jimmy Carter (1977–1981). From 1993 to 2001 during the Clinton administration, he was United States ambassador to the European Union; under secretary of commerce for international trade; under secretary of state for economic, business and agricultural affairs; and deputy secretary of the treasury. He served as special representative of the president and secretary of state on Holocaust-era issues, and helped provide belated justice to Holocaust survivors and other victims of Nazi oppression. He chronicled those experiences in his 2003 book, *Imperfect Justice: Looted Assets, Slave Labor, and the Unfinished Business of World War II.*

    An honors graduate of the University of North Carolina at Chapel Hill and of Harvard Law School, Eizenstat is currently the head of international trade and finance at the law firm of Covington & Burling in Washington, D.C., and serves on the boards of numerous corporate, academic, religious, and public policy institutions. He is married to Frances Eizenstat, and they have two married sons, Jay and Brian, and four grandchildren.

CHAPTER ONE

An American Hero of the Holocaust

For all its villains and victims, the history of the Holocaust also has its share of heroes, although painfully few. There were villagers who risked their lives by sheltering Jewish children. There were individuals such as Oskar Schindler and Raoul Wallenberg who protected Jews through an array of ruses. There were a handful of diplomats like Chiune Sugihara of Japan and Feng-Shan Ho of China who defied their superiors by granting visas to Jewish refugees.

There were even some Americans among the heroes of the Holocaust, although not many because the United States never came under Nazi occupation. Varian Fry, a young American journalist, traveled to Vichy France in 1940 to organize the escape of some 2,000 refugees with the help of a dissident U.S. consul, Hiram Bingham IV, a Unitarian minister from Massachusetts and his wife, Waitstill and Martha Sharp, and a handful of other courageous activists.

This book is about an American who was a different kind of hero of the Holocaust. Josiah E. DuBois, Jr., was not a rescuer or a shelterer. He was a whistle-blower.

DuBois did not risk his life in doing what he did. But he certainly risked his career. And that takes courage, a special kind of courage that not many people possess.

*   *   *

To understand the significance of what DuBois did, it is important first to consider the political and social environment in which he lived and worked during the 1930s and the early years of World War II.

DuBois was born and raised in Camden, New Jersey. His upbringing in the 1910s and 1920s offered no clues to the extraordinary courage and humanitarianism he would one day exhibit. He enjoyed a pleasant but nondescript childhood and adolescence, pursued his undergraduate studies at the University of Pennsylvania and then went on to its school of law, from which he graduated in 1934.

Josiah E. DuBois, Jr., at approximately the time of his graduation from the University of Pennsylvania Law School (1932).

DuBois came to adulthood during the tumultuous 1930s, when economic hardship, nativist sentiment, and anti-Semitism were important factors in shaping the U.S. policies that would affect Europe's Jews under Hitler—policies that DuBois would soon confront.

In 1933, at the worst point in the Depression, unemployment in the United States reached 25 percent. Even by 1938 it was still above 15 percent. These conditions stimulated a national mood of insecurity, fear, and anxiety, especially at the prospect that new immigrants would take jobs away from Americans. These fears became so entrenched that even during the 1940s, when war production eliminated unemployment, many Americans remained apprehensive that the Depression would return after the war.

Nativist attitudes, which were particularly widespread in the 1920s, persisted during the 1930s and 1940s. Many Americans disliked foreigners of any kind and wanted to end, or at least significantly reduce, the trickle of immigration that still existed. Job competition was only part of the reason; many Americans also harbored fears about the cultural impact foreigners had on the United States.

This intense resentment of foreigners was reinforced by an increasingly popular race-based view of human society. In the late 1800s and early 1900s, many Americans—like many Europeans—came under the sway of anthropologists and eugenicists on both continents who contended that Anglo-Saxons were biologically superior to other peoples.

Antisemitism on the Rise

At the same time, anti-Semitism, already on the rise in the 1920s, increased dramatically in the 1930s and reached its peak in American history in the late 1930s and the World War II years. The view that Jews constituted an undesirable race was widely accepted. There was also a substantial level of political anti-Semitism, that is, the view that a world Jewish conspiracy secretly wielded vast international economic and political power. Jews supposedly manipulated the capitalist system through their stranglehold on international finance and simultaneously controlled the Soviet Union as well as the international Communist movement and aspired to global domination. Although such theories as a whole were too extreme to gain general acceptance, parts of this mythology spread through American society; for instance, it was widely believed that Jews tended to be Communists or that they were capitalist manipulators who were to blame for bringing on the Depression.[1]

By 1940, there more than one hundred anti-Semitic organizations throughout the United States, most notably the Silver Shirts, the German–American Bund (American Nazis), and the Defenders of the Christian Faith. The most influential of the anti-Semitic demagogues was the Catholic priest Charles Coughlin, whose weekly radio broadcasts reached several million Americans.[2] Opinion polls from 1940 through 1945 indicated that about one-third of the American public was anti-Semitic. (This figure does not include individuals who harbored anti-Semitic sentiments but were reluctant to reveal them to those taking the polls.)[3] Twelve percent of those polled said they were prepared to support an anti-Semitic campaign, and an additional 20 percent expressed sympathy for such a movement. During the 1930s, and even more so during the 1940s, the rhetoric of hate turned into violence in Boston and New York City, where there were a number of instances of teenage gangs assaulting Jewish schoolchildren.[4]

Shutting America's Doors

These high levels of nativism and anti-Semitism provide the backdrop to U.S. government policy toward Europe's Jews. These attitudes had helped bring about the National Origins Immigration bills of 1921 and 1924, which virtually shut America's doors to immigrants.

Passed in 1921, the Johnson Immigration Act stipulated that the number of immigrants from any country during a given year could not exceed 3 percent of the number of immigrants from that country who had been living in the United States at the time of the 1910 national census. In other words, if there were 10,000 individuals of Irish origin living in the United States in 1910, the number of immigrants permitted from Ireland in any year would be a maximum of 300. In 1924, the immigration regulations were tightened even further: the percentage was reduced from 3 percent to 2 percent, and instead of the 1910 census, the quota numbers would be based on an earlier census, that of 1890.

The reason for tightening the restrictions was to reduce the number of Jews and Italian Americans, because the bulk of Jewish and Italian immigrants in the United States had arrived after 1890. Indeed, the original version of the Johnson Act had been submitted to Congress with a report by the chief of the United

States Consular Service, Wilbur Carr, that characterized would-be Jewish immigrants from Poland as "filthy, un-American, and often dangerous in their habits . . . lacking any conception of patriotism or national spirit."[5]

As the Nazi persecution of Jews intensified during the middle and late 1930s, the U.S. quota system functioned as its creators had intended: it kept out all but a handful of Jews. The annual quota for Germany and Austria (the two were combined in 1938), for example, was 27,370, and for Poland it was just 6,542.

Even those meager quota allotments were almost always unfilled. Zealous consular officials with few exceptions heeded the method proposed by Assistant Secretary of State Breckinridge Long to "put every obstacle in the way and to require additional evidence [that a would-be immigrant would not be a burden on America] and to resort to various administrative advices which would postpone and postpone and postpone the granting of the visas."[6] Prof. David S. Wyman called this deliberately designed bureaucratic maze "paper walls." These obstacles ensured that most Jewish refugees would remain far from America's shores.

The immigration quotas became law before Franklin D. Roosevelt was elected president in 1932, but he fully supported both the quota system that he inherited and the State Department's administration of it. Long, an old personal friend of Roosevelt's, kept the president informed of what he was doing to reduce immigration, and he received FDR's support. According to Long, Roosevelt confided to him in the autumn of 1940 that "when [refugee advocate James G. McDonald] started condemning and criticizing me [Long], the President told him not to 'pull any sob stuff' on him."[7]

During the period of the Nazi genocide, from late 1941 and until early 1945, only 10 percent of the already miniscule quotas from Axis-controlled European countries were actually filled. That means almost 190,000 quota places were unused—almost 190,000 lives that could have been saved even under the existing immigration restrictions.

It was not until more than two decades after World War II that the national origins quota system was finally abandoned. The passage of the Immigration Act of 1965 "lifted the shadow of racism from American immigration policy," as Prof. John Higham put it.[8] Tragically, it came twenty-five years too late for the millions of Jews trapped in Hitler's inferno.

Speaking Out against Hitler

Immigration was not the only way in which President Roosevelt might have taken steps to aid the Jews in Nazi Germany during the 1930s. For example, he could have spoken out publicly about their plight and thereby put pressure on the Hitler regime, which at least in its early years, was still interested in cultivating relations, especially economic relations, with the United States.

Some who met with FDR during Hitler's first year in power came away with the impression that Roosevelt intended to be outspoken. In the spring after 1933, shortly after Hitler's rise to power, James G. McDonald, who chaired the American Foreign Policy Association and was soon to be named League of Nations high commissioner for refugees, visited Germany. Upon his return to the United States, McDonald shared with the president his grim assessment of the status of German Jewry. McDonald told FDR "it would be desirable if some very frank speaking could be done to Hitler." Roosevelt replied "that he had a plan in mind to appeal over the head of Hitler to the German people," McDonald wrote at the time.[9] Judge Irving Lehman, the brother of New York's governor, had a similar experience when he visited the White House on September 14, 1933, together with longtime Roosevelt friend Henry Morgenthau, Jr. They asked the president to issue a

President Franklin D. Roosevelt, in 1933.

statement about Germany's Jews. Roosevelt said he preferred to make a statement about human rights abuses in Germany in general, without focusing on the Jews. But he did not do even that.

Throughout 1933, the president of the American Jewish Congress, Rabbi Stephen S. Wise, repeatedly asked administration officials to urge FDR to publicly deplore Hitler's treatment of the Jews. Those requests fell on deaf ears. In a private letter on October 18, an anguished Wise wrote that despite his many appeals, "We have had nothing but indifference and unconcern [from the White House] up to this time."[10]

Mindful of the electorate's fear of entanglement in foreign affairs, FDR made it clear that the United States would not intervene against the persecution of German Jews, except for the tiny minority who happened to hold American citizenship. Shortly after William E. Dodd was named U.S. ambassador to Germany in June 1933, he asked the president what position he should articulate in Berlin regarding the Jews. According to Dodd's diary, Roosevelt responded that it was "not a governmental affair. We can do nothing except for American citizens who happen to be made victims."[11]

Roosevelt held eighty-two press conferences in 1933. The subject of the persecution of the Jews arose only once, and then not because FDR raised it. A reporter asked, "Have any organizations asked you to act in any way in connection with the reported persecution of the Jews over in Germany by the Hitler government?" The president replied: "I think a good many of these have come in. They were all sent over to the Secretary of State."[12]

In fact, it would be five years and another 348 presidential press conferences before anything about Jewish refugees would be mentioned again by the president. Keenly attuned to the public's isolationist mood and the prevalence of anti-Semitic sentiment, FDR simply avoided mentioning the Jews. Even when the subject came up, it did not go far. Typical was a reporter's question on September 2, 1938, as to whether the president had any comment on Italy's order expelling 22,000 Jews. The president's reply: "No." During 998 press conferences over the course of his twelve years in office, FDR never delivered that "appeal to the German people" to which he had referred in his meeting with James McDonald in 1933.[13]

From Evian To Kristallnacht

While much of the American public and media was hostile to increased refugee immigration or U.S. involvement in European matters, a small but vocal group of Congressmen and newspaper columnists did raise their voices in protest in the late 1930s, especially following the extreme persecution of Jews and anti-Nazis accompanying Germany's annexation of Austria in March 1938. Fearing that such criticism would now become "exceedingly strong and prolonged," State Department officials decided the best way to elude the pressure for refugee action would be "to get out in front and attempt to guide it" by inviting thirty-two countries to send representatives to a conference in Evian, France, in July 1938.[14]

To assure both the American public and other governments that no country would be called upon to take in significant numbers of refugees, the administration's invitation and other pronouncements regarding the conference stressed that "no country would be expected or asked to receive a greater number of immigrants than is permitted by its existing legislation."[15] Moreover, the United States acquiesced in the British refusal to discuss Jewish refugee immigration to Mandatory Palestine, which England intended to restrict in order to appease Palestinian Arab rioters. As a result, the Evian conference concluded without offering anything remotely close to its declared aim of finding places to which substantial numbers of refugees could go.[16]

In the autumn of that year, Hitler's persecution of German Jewry took a new and violent turn with a nationwide government-sponsored pogrom on the night of November 9–10. The assault came to be known as *Kristallnacht* (Night of the Broken Glass), a reference to the enormous quantity of glass from the shattered windows of Jewish homes and businesses. An estimated one hundred Jews were murdered; tens of thousands were incarcerated in concentration camps; thousands of Jewish-owned businesses were demolished; and most of Germany's synagogues burned while firemen acted only to protect adjacent non-Jewish property.

President Roosevelt denounced the attacks, temporarily recalled the American ambassador from Germany, and announced that he would extend the visitor's permits of the 12,000–15,000 German refugees already in America so they would not have to return immediately to Germany. Regarding the possibility of relaxing the immigration laws, however, FDR said that was "not in contemplation."[17]

Nevertheless, some members of Congress did contemplate bringing more refugees to the United States. Inspired by the British example of the Kindertransport, which brought 10,000 German Jewish children to England during 1938–1939, members of Congress crafted the Wagner–Rogers bill, which proposed to admit 20,000 refugee children from Germany outside the quota system. It was introduced in early 1939. Although a number of prominent Americans supported the bill, they could not overcome vigorous lobbying by nativists and isolationists and the tide of public opinion, which still ran strongly against increasing immigration despite the German pogrom. The president's cousin, Laura Delano Houghteling, who was the wife of the U.S. commissioner of immigration, articulated the sentiment of many opponents of the bill when she remarked that "20,000 charming children would all too soon grow into 20,000 ugly adults."[18]

Ironically, there was considerably more public sympathy in the autumn of 1940, when *Pets* magazine sought temporary homes for purebred British puppies to avoid the German aerial bombardments of London. Several thousand readers offered to give them homes.

Meanwhile, just as the Wagner–Rogers Bill was being squelched in Congress, the refugee issue came to the fore once again as the German cruise ship *St. Louis*, carrying more than 900 Jewish refugees, was denied permission to land its passengers at Havana. The ship hovered off the coast of Florida for several days, its passengers hoping to be granted haven in the United States. Instead, the refugees were sent back to Europe.

America on the Verge of War

When the Nazis invaded and occupied Poland in September 1939, Hitler had not yet formulated his genocidal plans for the Jews. Options then under consideration by the Nazi hierarchy included the deportation of European Jews to the African island of Madagascar or, alternatively, the concentration of all captured Jews on a vast reservation in Poland's Lublin region. In the meantime, the German occupation authorities exploited the Jews in occupied Poland, stripping them of their possessions, conscripting them into forced-labor brigades, and using them as convenient targets for abusive German soldiers.

In early 1940, Hitler revived the medieval concept of forcing the Jews into walled ghettoes. The Jewish community of Warsaw, which had numbered 300,000 before the war but swelled to nearly 400,000 as refugees poured in from other parts of Poland, was confined to a section of the city that was soon ravaged by hunger, disease, and Nazi atrocities. Strict German limits on the amount of food that could enter the ghetto resulted in mass starvation. Extreme overcrowding in the ghetto's dwellings encouraged the spread of deadly diseases such as typhus. Many more Jews were murdered in random Nazi pogroms or were literally worked to death in forced-labor groups.

During the spring of 1940, as the German war machine stormed across Belgium, Denmark, the Netherlands, and France, a near-hysteria swept America concerning the danger of Nazi spies and saboteurs infiltrating the United States. It was fueled by rumors that Germany's shockingly swift conquest of France had been abetted by such internal subversion. The American media overflowed with stories of "Trojan Horses," "enemies within our gates," and "Hitler's slave spies in America."[19]

Although the threat of subversion was a legitimate concern and care certainly needed to be taken to keep out Nazi agents and collaborators, the administration went overboard in its reaction. Instead of adding reasonable screening precautions to the existing immigration procedures, the State Department exaggerated the threat, and Assistant Secretary of State Breckinridge Long used it as a pretext to cut in half the use of the already small quotas. In view of anti-immigration, antialien, and anti-Semitic attitudes then prevalent in the State Department, it is evident that the subversion issue was not the only factor driving the new policy.

That 50 percent cut in immigration in mid-1940 was not the last of Breckinridge Long's changes. In the months that followed, he and his State Department colleagues concluded that there was an increasing danger of foreign agents entering the United States disguised as refugees. In July 1941, Long further tightened visa procedures. Use of the quotas dropped to 25 percent, a total of about 15,000 immigrants per year.

Meanwhile, isolationism remained strong among the American public, sometimes spilling over into anti-Semitism. Aviation hero Charles Lindbergh speaking at an America First rally in September 1941, accused "the Jews" of "pressing this country toward war" and complained about what he called "their large ownership and influence in our motion pictures, our press, our radio and our government." It was a view shared by a frighteningly substantial segment of the American public, and Lindbergh's stature gave it added credibility.[20]

This, then, was the setting as Josiah DuBois entered government service. An America wracked by economic hardship, nativism, anti-Semitism, and isolationism was closing its doors ever tighter and hoping desperately to avoid involvement in Europe's conflicts. Yet at the same time, it was an America that was being drawn inexorably closer to that war because Hitler's appetite would not be satisfied by swallowing large parts of Europe. Global conquest was his ultimate aim, as a growing number of Americans slowly realized.

From 1936 to 1940, DuBois worked for stretches of time in the Treasury Department, including a brief stint in the department's Foreign Funds Control unit. As war between the United States and Germany became increasingly likely in 1941, the Foreign Funds Control team intensified its efforts to block German economic penetration of the Americas. DuBois was invited to return to the unit, and he accepted.

The Holocaust Begins

With the German invasion of the Soviet Union in June 1941, the German policy of encouraging Jewish emigration through severe discrimination and occasional violence changed to one of mass murder. Special mobile killing units (*Einsatzgruppen*) operating directly behind the front lines began systematically to slaughter the hundreds of thousands of Jews in the newly conquered areas of the USSR. For the most part, the method was mass gunfire, carried out at the sides of ditches that the victims themselves had been forced to dig. By the end of 1942, the Einsatzgruppen had killed an estimated 1.4 million Jews in eastern Poland, the Baltic states, and the western Soviet Union.[21] During the winter of 1941–1942, the first death camps, equipped with gas chambers, were established in occupied Poland. In January 1942, the Nazi officers in charge of implementing the Holocaust met in the Berlin suburb of Wannsee to coordinate their strategy: the Jews would be shipped by train to the camps in Poland. In the next three years, about 3 million Jews from across Europe were deported, mostly via freight train, to the killing centers to be put to death in the gas chambers.

Scattered information about the mass killings began arriving in the West in the late summer and early fall of 1941. It reached the Allied governments and, to a lesser extent, the mass media, through sources such as diplomats from neutral countries who were stationed in the Reich and journalists in the region who were able to pick up bits and pieces. The State Department gathered the information but for many months treated it with a somewhat skeptical eye. In part, the State Department's doubts were fueled by memories of World War I atrocity stories that had later proved false. But to some extent the doubts were also the product of anti-Jewish prejudice among some State Department officials. They tended to instinctively suspect that Jewish sources exaggerated the suffering of their coreligionists in order to gain sympathy or political advantage.

At the same time, however, many reports about the mass killings were reaching Jewish organizations in the United States, and Jewish leaders began pressing the State Department for confirmation. A turning point came in mid-August 1942, when the State Department received strong evidence that the killings were not random massacres but part of a systematic program of mass annihilation. After persuading Rabbi Stephen Wise, president of the American Jewish Congress, to withhold the information from the public until it could be further verified, Undersecretary of State Sumner Welles took three more months before deciding that it was verified to his satisfaction.

On December 17, 1942, Great Britain, the United States, the Soviet Union, and eight other nations issued the Allied War Crimes Declaration. The statement condemned Germany's policy of extermination of the Jews and pledged that the perpetrators would be brought to justice. It is noteworthy that the first draft of the statement, prepared by British officials, referred to "reports from Europe which leave no room for doubt" that genocide was under way. The State Department objected to that phrase on the grounds that it would "expose [the Allies] to increased pressure from all sides to do something more specific in order to aid these people." The wording in the final draft was watered down to "numerous reports from Europe."[22]

Despite their verbal condemnation of the mass murder, neither the British nor the American government was willing to attempt to rescue Jews. The British believed any significant flow of Jews out of Axis-occupied Europe would place great pressure on them to reverse their policy of tightly restricting Jewish immigration to Palestine. They had established this closed-doors policy in the White Paper of 1939 in response to Palestinian Arab violence and were unwilling to modify it in the years that followed. The Roosevelt administration, for its part, feared a large-scale exodus of Jews from Nazi Europe because that would put pressure on the United States to open its doors, at least to some extent. U.S. officials insisted that the only way to rescue the Jews was through victory on the battlefield. "Nothing can be done to save these helpless unfortunates except through the invasion of Europe, the defeat of the German army, and the breaking of the German power," Assistant Secretary Adolph Berle insisted. "There is no other way."[23] "Rescue through victory" was little more than camouflage for the real policy of both governments, which was in fact to avoid rescue opportunities.

At a March 1943 meeting at the White House between British Foreign Minister Anthony Eden, President Roosevelt, Secretary of State Cordell Hull, and several other officials, Hull raised the issue of perhaps helping the 60,000 Jews in Bulgaria. Eden replied "that the whole problem of the Jews in Europe is very difficult and that we should move very cautiously about offering to take all Jews out of a country like Bulgaria. If we do that, then the Jews of the world will be wanting us to make similar offers in Poland and Germany."[24] No one at the meeting questioned Eden's position. On another occasion, a British official expressed opposition to the rescue of Jewish refugees because of the "difficulties of disposing of any considerable number of Jews, should they be rescued."[25]

In a similar vein, a State Department official in 1943 described the problem this way: "There was always the danger that the German Government might agree to turn over to the United States and to Great Britain a large number of Jewish refugees. . . . In the event of our admission of inability to take care of these people, the onus for their continued persecution would have been largely transferred from the German Government to the Allied nations."[26] Likewise, a May 1943 memo by State Department official Robert Alexander opposed rescuing refugees on the grounds that it would "take the burden and the curse off Hitler."[27] His colleague R. Borden Reams bluntly characterized as a "danger" the possibility that the Nazis "might agree to turn over to the United States and to Great Britain a large number of Jewish refugees."[28]

In early 1943, confronted with increasing calls for action from refugee advocates, lawmakers, and the press in both Great Britain and the United States, the British Foreign Office and the State Department decided to hold a conference on the refugee issue. Its ostensible purpose was to find ways to rescue Jews, but in fact it was a way of avoiding rescue. Neither the British nor the Americans were willing to host the meeting in their own capital lest the event prove to be a magnet for refugee advocates. They announced their intention to hold it in Ottawa, but in their haste to find a city in another country they had neglected to inform the Canadians. When the Canadian government objected, the conference was relocated to a more remote site that would be inaccessible to Jewish protesters and the media: the island of Bermuda.

After twelve days of meetings in April 1943, representatives of the two governments announced that their decisions had to remain secret because "knowledge of the recommendations . . . would be of aid or comfort to our enemies."[29] In reality, the Bermuda Conference recommended almost nothing in the way of rescue proposals. Nevertheless, its real objective was accomplished: it undermined the pressures for action by giving the appearance of planning steps to rescue Jews.

It was at this point in the spring of 1943 that the plight of Europe's Jews came within the purview of Josiah DuBois and his Treasury colleagues, for reasons to be discussed later. During the events of the previous years, DuBois had no discernible knowledge of, or interest in, Jewish affairs, a fact that makes his heroism all the more unlikely and his story all the more intriguing. He stepped unknowingly onto the stage of history—but once there, he rose to the heights of moral courage.

Notes

1. For more on anti-Semitism in America in the 1930s, see Charles H. Stember, *Jews in the Mind of America* (New York: Basic Books, 1966).

2. For more on Father Coughlin, see Donald Warren, *Radio Priest: Charles Coughlin, the Father of Hate Radio* (New York: The Free Press, 1996).

3. David S. Wyman, *The Abandonment of the Jews: America and the Holocaust, 1941–1945* (New York: Pantheon, 1984), 14–15.

4. Stephen H. Norwood, "Marauding Youth and the Christian Front: Antisemitic Violence in Boston and New York During World War II," *American Jewish History* 91:2 (June 2003), 233–267.

5. Richard Breitman and Alan M. Kraut, *American Refugee Policy and European Jewry, 1933–1945* (Bloomington and Indianapolis: Indiana University Press, 1987), 32.

6. David S. Wyman, *Paper Walls: America and the Refugee Crisis, 1938–1941* (University of Massachusetts Press, 1968), 173.

7. Wyman 1968, 147.

8. John Higham, *Send These to Me: Jews and Other Immigrants in Urban America* (New York: Atheneum, 1975), 64.

9. Diary of James G. McDonald, entry for 1 May 1933, United States Holocaust Memorial Museum, Washington, D.C.

10. Wise to Julian W. Mack, 18 October 1933, in Carl Hermann Voss, ed. *Stephen S. Wise: Servant of the People—Selected Letters* (Philadelphia: Jewish Publication Society of America), 195.

11. William E. Dodd, Jr., and Martha Dodd, eds., *Ambassador Dodd's Diary* (New York: Harcourt Brace and Company, 1941), 5.

12. Laurel Leff and Rafael Medoff, "New Documents Shed More Light on FDR's Holocaust Failure," *American Jewish World*, 30 April 2004, 5.

13. Ibid.

14. Wyman 1968, 44.

15. Ibid., 43.

16. Wyman (ibid., 43–51) quotes internal State Department documents showing that the Roosevelt administration's decision to hold the conference was motivated not by a sincere desire to find havens for refugees but merely in order to "get out in front and attempt to guide" the growing pressure from liberal members of Congress and the press to address the refugee crisis. Also see Paul R. Bartrop, ed., *False Havens: The British Empire and the Holocaust,* Studies in the Shoah, vol. 10 (Lanham, MD: University Press of America, 1995), 53–78.

17. Ibid.

18. Breitman and Kraut, 74.

19. Wyman 1968, 185–186.

20. Stember, op. cit.

21. Raul Hilberg, *The Destruction of the European Jews* (New York: Harper & Row, 1961), 256.

22. Wyman 1984, 75.

23. Cited in Monty N. Penkower, *The Jews Were Expendable: Free World Diplomacy and the Holocaust* (Urbana and Chicago: University of Illinois Press, 1983), 330, n37.

24. Wyman 1984, 97.

25. Ibid., 98.

26. Ibid., 99.

27. Ibid.

28. Ibid.

29. Ibid., 119.

CHAPTER TWO

The Struggle for U.S. Rescue Action

When Josiah DuBois began working in the Treasury Department in 1935, the last thing he expected was that it would involve him in the affairs of Europe's Jews. Even after he returned, in 1940, to the Treasury after a hiatus, and was assigned to combat Nazi economic penetration of the Western Hemisphere, he had little inkling as to what lay ahead. It seemed to be an ordinary government job. It would soon turn out to be anything but.

I. The Early Years

Q:[1] Perhaps you could tell us to begin, something about how you happened to achieve [your] career in the civil government?

DuBois: Well, I graduated from the University of Pennsylvania law school in '34 and was granted a fellowship and worked under Dean Goodrich of the law school for one year. . . . Thereafter, the Dean, actually unbeknownst to me, recommended me to the Treasury Department. . . . They were looking for young lawyers. I was interviewed and granted the job, and I worked in the Treasury for two and a half years, actually, on, initially, the problems relating to gold. As you may recall, they had withdrawn gold coins, which created a lot of problems . . . [In] the summer of '38 . . . I resigned and came back here to work with my brother, Herbert, who is one of the partners now in this firm. . . . [In] 1940, I got a call from one of the lawyers that I had worked with in the Treasury asking if I could come down there to Washington to assist them in work known later as the Foreign Funds Control. It involved, actually, what you might call the beginning of preparation of economic warfare directed against Germany.

[In 1941], they sent me with one other person from the State Department on a two-man mission to Central America. We went to every country in Central America and the idea of our mission, basically, was to try to get the Central American countries to do what we had done, namely (to oversimplify it), freeze all accounts in which the Germans had any kind of an interest, direct or indirect, so that they couldn't use the moneys in those accounts for espionage, sabotage, and spying activities in this country. . . .

[Once] they sent me to North Africa. That was about a five or six months' mission. . . . [T]he main function was the Treasury had issued, or were issuing, this gold seal currency, which you've probably heard about, which they used in North Africa. And the main idea of that, of course, was to dry up the currency which we felt the Germans had more or less secreted in North Africa, and rather than to permit that to be used in connection with our operations we wanted our own currency; and a lot of my legal work had to do with that.

[W]e arrived [in Algiers] within less than a month after the [November 1942] invasion [by the Allies]. I'll never forget, the very first day I was there they put me in a temporary hotel, and the German planes were still coming over and one of them hit a hotel right across the street from me. It scared the s— out of me! A night or two later, I was attending some kind of a cocktail party or something, with Bernie Bernstein and a few others, and there was a porch out there. I heard these planes roaring and I wanted to see what was going on. I just walked out on the porch and looked up. Bernie came out and grabbed me by the collar, "What are you doing, are you crazy, standing out there?" I wasn't thinking.

*   *   *

It was during DuBois's stay in Algiers that he first encountered the Roosevelt administration's unsympathetic response to the plight of Jewish refugees. Under the pro-Vichy regime that ruled North Africa from mid-1940 until the Allied conquest, more than four thousand Jews were interned in dozens of forced labor camps along the Morocco–Algeria border. The prisoners included Jews who had fled Nazi Europe but were unable to secure visas to reach the West, Algerian Jews involved in the local anti-Vichy underground, and various political prisoners. Following the Allied capture of the region, President Roosevelt allowed the pro-Vichy regime of Francois Giraud to remain in power, and even its Office of Jewish Affairs, which had been in charge of implementing anti-Jewish legislation and shipping Jews to labor camps, continued to operate. At the same time, FDR announced that he had "requested the liberation of all persons in Northern Africa who had been imprisoned because they opposed the efforts of the Nazis" and had "asked for the abrogation of all laws and decrees inspired by Nazi governments."

Given to understand that the refugees would be released promptly if funds were made available to cover their initial expenses, the American Jewish Joint Distribution Committee—the main U.S. Jewish agency for direct refugee relief—sought, and received, permission from the Treasury Department to provide 2 million francs to support the first 1,500 refugees to be set free. In Algiers on January 18, 1943, DuBois met with U.S. Consul General Samuel Wiley to follow up on the Joint's effort.

DuBois was disappointed to discover that the refugees would not be quickly freed and that Wiley was among those opposing a speedy release. DuBois pointed out to Wiley that the administration was already being strongly criticized in the U.S. press because of its acquiescence in the continued rule of the pro-Vichy authorities. Excerpts from DuBois's account of the meeting:

*   *   *

When I asked Wiley how long he thought it would take before the refugees would be released he replied three or four months; that a considerable study of the problems involved would have to be made.

I expressed to Mr. Wiley my failure to understand why it was taking so long to solve a problem which it seemed so important to solve as rapidly as possible; that he knew probably better than I the great amount of criticism which had been leveled at [the U.S. government's] position in this matter; that this type of criticism tended to hurt the war effort; and that it would seem to me that it would pay solely from the standpoint of the war effort for the Allies to spend a certain amount of time, effort and money to solve the problem without delay. Wiley agreed that considerable criticism had been leveled and that the problem should be solved as soon as possible but claimed the solution was difficult and would take time.

I questioned him about the possibility of having the Army hire these refugees as they were hiring the Arabs. Wiley stated that the possibility of placing them in labor battalions had been discussed but the British had finally turned it down. I explained that I was not speaking of regimentation but of voluntary employment. Wiley indicated that there should not be such concern over regimentation; that Americans were being conscripted every day. I explained why I thought the democratic method of selective service was different from telling a group of prisoners that their "choice" was to remain in prison or go in the Army. Wiley then stated that the voluntary employment of the refugees differed from the employment of Arabs in that if the Army no longer needed the Arabs they could go back to their former way of life; and that there was also the problem of finding a place for the refugees to live. I voiced the view that it would be worth the effort and expense to hire the refugees even if they did not put in a full day's work "earning their money" and to supply them with living quarters; that even if they slept in pup tents they would probably enjoy life more and from our selfish point of view we would at least avoid the harmful criticism.

Wiley stated that there had been so much criticism of things done that "they" (he and others) were becoming "hard skinned" about it and that "the only guide was whether or not their conscience was clear about this and similar matters." I expressed the view that the test should not be one's conscience in issues such as this but what was best in the interests of the war effort.

* * *

In the months to follow, most of the prisoners were indeed released and either enlisted in the British army or were given jobs on local U.S. or British army bases. Whether DuBois's protest to Wiley influenced that policy is unclear.[2]

II. Working at the Treasury

Creative young attorneys like DuBois found a welcome environment in the Treasury Department under Henry Morgenthau, Jr. DuBois's fellow staff members Edward Bernstein and John Pehle; Morgenthau's sons, Robert and Henry III; and

Jewish rescue activist Hillel Kook (better known as Peter Bergson) recall Secretary Morgenthau and the atmosphere in the department:

EDWARD BERNSTEIN:[3] The Treasury was a unique place in many respects. First, it had a Secretary of the Treasury who was eager to find new ideas for the government. New ideas for the government during the Depression, new ideas for the government once it had begun to resist the dictators in Europe. And he had a group of men there who were encouraged to think. And if you tell people to think and they are smart, they are going to come up with ideas. And they did.

This was as good a collection of people at the Treasury as I have ever known. Good in the sense that they were bright, innovative, and unafraid. And they went ahead and they told the Secretary of the Treasury just what they thought he ought to do. And the Secretary was very receptive and unafraid, and he did do what had to be done.

* * *

JOHN PEHLE:[4] Henry Morgenthau was a first-class person to work for. He gathered around him young people who were very devoted to the work being done, who were very bright, very energetic. And backed them up. He was very open in what was going on. He would go to a Cabinet meeting and come back and call the group the "9:30 group" which was the top people in the Treasury into his office and tell them exactly what had gone on. Many Cabinet officials did the opposite—they didn't tell their subordinates anything about what happened. So it was a very interesting, challenging thing to work for him.

* * *

HILLEL KOOK:[5] [W]hen somebody told me they could get me in to see Henry Morgenthau [in 1943], I went to see him and told him about the need for governmental action [to rescue European Jews] . . . Anyway, he was a very coolheaded man and I remember my first meeting with him was painful because he sat there very quietly, stone-faced, and I didn't know whether he was listening or not. He was terribly punctual. I remember for our second meeting set for twelve o'clock, I arrived about five minutes late. I was actually in the building earlier but it took longer than usual to get through the guards. So they were already sitting in the room talking—there were Joe DuBois and John Pehle and another man. I apologized for being late and he was even more serious, more long-faced.

After a little while he sneezed and his secretary said "God bless you," but he didn't hear it. While I was talking, he excused himself and said, seriously, that nobody had said "God bless you." His secretary told him that she had, and he said that he didn't hear her. So I told him it was not important if he had heard her, only if God had heard her. He smiled and the ice was broken. That was my introduction to those three people who did some important work later. They became the three top executives in the War Refugee Board. Pehle was the executive director. And they told me that in the years they worked with Morgenthau, they had never seen him converted to anything in such a way. He withstood pressure from all directions despite the fact that he was a relative of the Lehmans who were opposed to this activity.[6]

* * *

HENRY MORGENTHAU III:[7] The chemistry between the 30-year-old youngster [DuBois] and my old man was immediate. My father was impressed by Joe's quick thinking, brilliance, his passion, his enthusiasm and his idealism. Joe, for his part, was thrilled as a young man by the responsibility that was thrust upon his shoulders and given to him on his mission.

* * *

ROBERT MORGENTHAU:[8] [My father] had a genius for identifying and picking good people who were creative and

Secretary of the Treasury Henry Morgenthau, Jr., in the 1930s.

imaginative and committed to the public service. And he had an extraordinary staff of fairly young, talented people. And I think he also had created the atmosphere where they were willing to come forward and tell him what they thought and how it should be done. And I think they, you know, they knew how he felt about the refugee problem. But they certainly played a key role in formulating the ideas and then putting them into practice. Just as some of those people and others helped create the whole Lend-Lease program.

* * *

PEHLE:[9] The State Department and the Treasury Department were both old-line agencies but when the New Deal came, the Treasury changed. The Department, because of Secretary Morgenthau, partly because of the influx of new young lawyers who were anxious to carry out New Deal programs. And the State Department, although there were some sections of the State Department that were new and liberal-minded, refugee problems tended to be handled by the old-line agencies that didn't really focus on refugee problems as a top priority.

Q: Was it anti-Semitic?

PEHLE: I wouldn't call the State Department an anti-Semitic organization but people have often thought, people in the State Department who deal with refugees had some anti-Semitism in their background. Breckinridge Long, Assistant Secretary of State, was a man who was a point man on refugee problems, and he had a reputation of not being favorably disposed to action in these areas.[10] . . .

We had a lot of young lawyers who were very anxious to improve the world. And didn't necessarily confine their thoughts to things that were strictly Treasury but would advance other ideas. This was sort of anathema to the State Department. And we tended just to reach opposite conclusions with most things that came up. Some people felt that if the State Department took the position, the Treasury naturally took the opposite position. But I don't think it was quite that bad.

* * *

BERNSTEIN:[11] [T]he anti-Semitism in the State Department, it was really built in, I would say, in the structure of the department. Individuals in the State Department might have been very friendly to Jews. . . . But if you went beyond individuals and those who administered the business of the State Department, there was a clear anti-Semitic environment. Nobody would have been willing to do anything that required out-of-the-ordinary, even listening to the problems and finding a solution to them. That's what you were confronted with especially in the immigration law section.

In 1940, when I came to the Treasury and first began to have business with the State Department, everybody understood that the State Department was on the extreme edge of the anti-Semitic environment in Washington. And I could see [from] the documents passing through my hands, that there was no hope of getting any help from them. The one place where the State Department could have been helpful to the Jews who were being at risk for their very lives in Germany, that was the part of the State Department which was most anti-Semitic.

The State Department, in restricting immigration of Jews, the first thing to bear in mind is, there was a lot of leeway as to how many visas would be issued. And who was entitled to a visa. I would say the State Department in general would have been very narrow in interpreting who was entitled to a visa. I think in the case of Jews they were much worse. They were—there was a problem that the proof had to be super great for them to agree to a visa for a Jew.

Q: Was it a "they aren't our kind" attitude?

BERNSTEIN: That's exactly the point . . . The State Department probably had a greater degree of anti-Semitism than other [departments], and particularly in the immigration section, because they felt the Jews were not like them. We didn't fit into how they thought the State Department and the U.S. economy ought to work.

III. The Treasury Department and the Holocaust

DuBois:[12] [During 1942,] the State Department had been receiving shocking information concerning what was going on in Europe with respect to the murder of the Jewish people. [This included a cable in] August of 1942, from the secretary of the World Jewish Congress in Switzerland, who reported that Hitler had under consideration a plan to exterminate all Jews in German-controlled Europe:

> Received alarming report that in Fuhrer's headquarters plan discussed and under consideration according to which all Jews in countries occupied or controlled Germany numbering 3½–4 millions should after deportation and concentration in East be exterminated at one blow to resolve once for all

the Jewish Question in Europe stop the action reported planned for autumn methods under discussion including prussic acid stop we transmit information with all reservation as exactitude cannot be confirmed stop informant stated to have close connections with highest German authorities and his reports generally speaking reliable.

The source of the cable was Gerhart Riegner, the World Jewish Congress representative in Switzerland:[13]

RIEGNER:[14] A German industrialist who was at the head of an enormous enterprise, was working for the war effort in Germany, had access to Hitler's headquarters. And in the summer of 1942 he heard at Hitler's headquarters a story according to which there was a plan under consideration to deport the totality of European Jewry to the East, eastern Europe, and to exterminate the totality, to kill the totality of European Jews after their deportation. This man, who was a very decent human being, considered that it was his duty to convey this report to the outside world. And he looked for an occasion to come to Switzerland, where he had friends, business friends, with whom he was in contact.

And he arrived somewhere in the end of July 1942 and approached his business friends with this message. And these business friends called in the press secretary of the Federation of Jewish Communities in Switzerland, who was a good friend of mine, who heard a story and said, well this is a matter that goes beyond the Swiss Jewish community, so we have to call in Dr. Riegner of the World Jewish Congress, who is in contact with America, with Britain, and with the outside world. So he called me in. The next day I met him, and he told me the whole story. . . .[15]

To imagine that human beings are capable of such action—it took me two days to convince myself of the possibility. I must say that I was helped by two facts: during the month of July, there was taking place all over western Europe, mass arrests of Jews in the streets of Paris, of Frankfurt, of Amsterdam, of Brussels, of Lyons, all over Western Europe. And we knew that these people were arrested and were transported to the East. We knew also that already before, a large action of deportation towards the East had been started in Germany, in Czechoslovakia, in Austria, and other places. So this story, for the first time, made concert, rational concert to all these individual happenings which were reported from various places. You could put them together and pin them down to a unique plan.

The second thing that was important in this respect was that the character of the German assassins, the German Gestapo, was a fact that was of course very well known to us. . . . In 1939, when Hitler invaded Poland, the first months, in September, October, we had terrible reports of mass killings. . . . So the brutality and the possibility of killings in large numbers in cities was known. . . .

Q: So what did you do once this industrialist had told you?

RIEGNER: I decided that I should convey this both to the American and British governments. And I went to see the American Consul and the British

Consul in Geneva and I said to them the following: this is what I heard from a very reliable source.... [H]e had brought other messages before which proved absolutely accurate. So I said to the Americans and the British, "Please inform your governments of this message. Please verify the message through your own secret services.... And third, please give the following message to Dr. Stephen Wise[16]... and to Mr. Sidney Silverman who was then [a Member of Parliament and] at the head of the British section of the World Jewish Congress in England. And I sent two identical messages, [but] to the British message I added, "please inform New York." Why, I can't tell you. I must have had some premonition that my message to Dr. Wise wouldn't be delivered.... [T]he State Department [did not] deliver [it] to Dr. Wise because of its "obviously unsubstantiated character"... [but] the British Foreign Office had contacted Sidney Silverman and given him the message. Sidney Silverman immediately cabled... to [Wise, in] New York.... And Dr. Wise... went to the State Department... and Sumner Welles[17] told [him], "Don't publish it now."

*　*　*

DuBois:[18] [B]y November of '42, sufficient information had been received that Sumner Welles authorized the Jewish organizations to make this public.... Then apparently the State Department felt that all of this information coming to the American people was causing too much pressure to be put upon the American [government,] upon the State Department to take action, that they decided to prevent... the furnishing of this information.

*　*　*

PEHLE:[19] The suppressing of the information was the key to action being taken on behalf of the refugees. If you don't know what's going on, and you suppress the information, the government becomes an accomplice to what the Nazis were doing, by hiding the information from the American public.

Q: Why did State do that?

PEHLE: Well I suppose the State Department felt that this was going to stir up a lot of people and that the main thing was to win the war and take care of these problems later. If anybody existed.

*　*　*

Under ordinary circumstances, matters involving Jewish refugees would not have come to the attention of Treasury Department officials such as DuBois. But in the spring of 1943, Gerhart Riegner asked the World Jewish Congress in New York to provide funds to facilitate the rescue of Jews from Rumania and France. Because sending funds into enemy territory was legally prohibited, the WJC required a special license from the Treasury Department to carry out the transaction. Treasury quickly approved it, but the State Department's long delays in agreeing to the license prompted DuBois and his colleagues to investigate State's handling of refugee rescue issues, resulting in a series of disturbing discoveries.

*　*　*

Q:[20] [H]ow did [the State Department] decide to prevent [the transmission of atrocity reports]?

DuBois: Well, specifically in a cable dated January 21, 1943, cable number 482—that number becomes significant—Riegner, who was the Secretary of the World Jewish Congress in Switzerland, relayed information to the State Department which described a horrible situation concerning the plight of the Jews in Europe. According to one source [that he cited], 6,000 Jews were being killed daily. The Jews were required before execution to strip themselves of all clothing and deprived of food. In Rumania, 130,000 Jews were deported to Transnistria. About 60,000 had already died and the remaining 70,000, according to the report, were starving. Disease was prevalent and the cable begged for assistance.

The State Department replied to that cable [number 354] with what on its surface would appear to be a most interested and innocuous cable. It said, "Your 482, January 21: In the future, we would suggest that you do not accept reports submitted to you to be transmitted to private persons in the United States unless such action is advisable because of extraordinary circumstance. Such private messages circumvent neutral country censorship, and it is felt by sending them we risk the possibility that they would necessarily be taken by neutral countries to curtail our means of communication."

Although this cable [354] on its face is most innocuous, when read together with the previous cable [482], it is nothing less than attempt at suppression of information by this government concerning the murder of the Jews.

This cable [354] was initialed by . . . Atherton[21] and Dunn,[22] Durbrow[23] and Hickerson,[24] and although the cable was signed for [Secretary of State Cordell] Hull by Sumner Welles, it is significant that there is not a word in the cable that would suggest that it was designed to prevent the furnishing of information concerning the extermination of the Jews.

* * *

DuBois became aware of these controversial cables because as he reviewed the file of materials relating to the license request he found a cable that mentioned 354, yet 354 itself was not in the file. He asked for a copy. In a later memo, he described what happened next:

We were advised that this cable did not relate to any matters that concerned the Treasury; that it had been seen by only a few people in the State Department; and that it could not be furnished to the Treasury. Thereafter

Josiah DuBois at work, in the 1940s.

I called Donald Hiss[25] [at the] State Department, (over a week ago) and requested that if possible, he get me a copy of this cable. Several days later I again called Donald Hiss, at his home, and he advised me that he was having considerable difficulty getting a copy of this cable [354] and the cable to which it referred [482] and that he would let me know as soon as he was able to get copies. Today I received a call from Donald Hiss's office requesting that, if possible, I be in his office at 2:30 inasmuch as he had something to speak to me about.[26]

*   *   *

DOROTHY DuBOIS:[27] [Joe] used to drive to work with a man named Donald Hiss and we were friends with the Hiss boys. Donald told my husband that the file [with the cables] was sitting right on his desk and that nobody was allowed to take it out of the office, but that he (Hiss) was going to lunch at some time of the day that day and the file would still be on the middle of his desk.

*   *   *

DuBois's account continues:[28]

When I saw Hiss this afternoon he gave me the signed copies of cable 354 and a previous cable to which 354 referred, a cable of January 21, 482. In showing me these cables Hiss stated that it had been made clear to him that cable 354 was none of Treasury's business and that in no event should it be shown to Treasury. He added that if it were known that he had shown me this cable he might well lose his job. (At this point he also mentioned that he was confident that his telephone was tapped and that others listened in on conversations which he had with Treasury officials.)

*   *   *

Q:[29] So what did Joe do?
    DOROTHY DuBOIS: He read the file, took notes and went back to his office. He was in a rage.

*   *   *

RICHARD C. GOODWIN:[30] As Joe dug deeper, he started making enemies. He told me of State Department officials who would say to him things like, "You Jews are a pain in the ass," because they assumed he was Jewish which, of course, he was not. The situation even became threatening. Joe told me that on one occasion a State Deparment official pulled him aside and said, "DuBois, you're heading for a lot of trouble, more than you can handle. You better drop this whole issue." If they thought that would scare him off, they didn't know Joe Dubois. Not only was he not intimidated, he saw it as an indication that he was on the right track. It convinced him that there must be even more skeletons in the closet, and it energized him to work even harder."

*   *   *

DuBOIS:[31] So [Morgenthau] arranged for a meeting with Hull and [Assistant Secretary of State] Breckinridge Long. Breckinridge Long, incidentally, was—
    Q: Anti-Semitic.

DuBois: Yes, I would say that's a good word to describe him. He was an anti-Semite.

* * *

Q:[32] Breckinridge Long—what was he like?

CELLER:[33] Well, I would say he was cold and austere, stiff as a poker, highly diplomatic in dress and in speech. He didn't seem to me one whom I could rely upon. He seemed to be far away as far as humanity is concerned. . . . [H]e was the least sympathetic to refugees of all the members of the State Department.

I met with him a number of times in the State Department and at various functions, receptions. . . . [When] I talked to him about the problem of refugees . . . he would say that he was very sorry about Hitler's action against the Jews, but as it was he shed a lot of crocodile tears, but in his capacity as an official of the State Department he did practically nothing to help rescue them. As a matter of fact, not only did he do nothing to rescue them, but he set up bottlenecks against the entry of Jews into the U.S. as refugees. . . .

Long said that he refused to grant visas for security reasons. Well, what is meant by security reasons—he felt that if he granted a visa to a refugee, the relative of the refugee might be held as a hostage in Germany, and . . . they might force him to behave in a way that involved the security of the United States and therefore he would not grant him a visa. Which was a lot of hooey. Utterly false reasoning. Nothing like that could have happened.

* * *

Q:[34] What do you think were the reasons the State Department didn't move fast and didn't want people to know [about the Holocaust]?

DuBois: Well, there's a combination of reasons. One of them is that there unquestionably were a number of anti-Semites in the State Department, and I know that personally. The second is, the normal attitude of the State Department in those days, and I suspect it still exists, that you don't do anything to rock the boat. You keep things calm. And the fact that the millions of Jews were being murdered while they were delaying, I don't think troubled most of them, frankly.

* * *

At the same time, the State Department had repeatedly delayed giving its approval to the requested license to transfer funds to aid French and Rumanian Jews. One of State's primary explanations for the delay was that it was seeking to clarify Britain's position on the proposed

Breckinridge Long, in the 1930s.

transfer of funds. At a December 17, 1943 staff meeting, DuBois and his colleagues Randolph Paul and Ansel Luxford expressed their exasperation at the consequences of the ongoing delays:[35]

MR. LUXFORD: I think it is important, too, in this field, to keep in mind this isn't a choice of the British saying "no action" and our saying "action." The British by doing nothing, are condemning these people to death.

MR. PAUL: I don't know how many of them have died so far.

MR. LUXFORD: That is right. Inaction here is a positive action to that end.

MR. DUBOIS: The British say condemn them to death, and we say they should get out.

MR. PAUL: I don't know how we can blame the Germans for killing them when we are doing this. The law calls them para-delicto, of equal guilt.

＊ ＊ ＊

During a series of meetings between Morgenthau and his aides during the last two weeks of December 1943, a division of opinion began to emerge as to what action they should take on the rescue issue. Morgenthau believed that Secretary of State Hull was basically sympathetic to the plight of the refugees but had unknowingly allowed policy to be determined by his deputies, such as Breckinridge Long. He thought that once Hull was alerted to the details of the situation, the disputed license would be granted, and refugee policy would significantly improve. But the Treasury aides, particularly DuBois and Luxford, were convinced that disinterest in the Jewish refugees was endemic in the State Department and would not end unless the refugee issue were taken completely out of the hands of State and assigned to a new government agency that would focus exclusively on rescue.

The idea of a special rescue agency first had been publicized by a Jewish political action committee known as the Bergson Group (after its leader, Palestine emissary Hillel Kook, who operated under the pseudonym Peter Bergson). Since February 1943, the group had been promoting this idea through public rallies, dozens of full-page newspaper advertisements, a dramatic march by 400 rabbis to the White House just before Yom Kippur, and meetings with Members of Congress and Roosevelt administration officials, including Secretary Morgenthau, DuBois, and Pehle. The group initially urged the Allies to establish "an inter-governmental committee" to rescue Jews from the Nazis."[36] *By July, the Bergson Group had refined its proposal by calling for creation of a specifically American, rather than Allied, agency. As will be seen below, this demand led*

Secretary of State Cordell Hull.

to the introduction of a Congressional resolution asking President Roosevelt to es-
tablish a rescue agency. The resolution, drafted by the Bergson Group and intro-
duced by Senator Guy Gillette (D-Iowa) and Rep. Will Rogers, Jr. (D-California),
was under active consideration in the House of Representatives and the Senate in
November and December, 1943.

Meanwhile, unbeknownst to the Bergson Group, a young staff lawyer at the
Foreign Economic Administration, Milton Handler, had drafted a somewhat simi-
lar proposal. It was circulated within the administration under the name of Han-
dler's friend and colleague, Assistant Solicitor General Oscar Cox. But, as Handler
later recalled, the proposal ran into "blank walls," leading the frustrated Handler to
"abandon the project"—until Morgenthau caught wind of it.[37] In December 1943,
in the midst of his discussions with his aides about the rescue problem, Morgenthau
invited Cox to join the discussion and outline his proposal.

What follows are excerpts from the minutes of two meetings on December
18 and 19, 1943, at which the rescue agency idea was put forward, first by DuBois
and Pehle and then by Cox, while at the same time Morgenthau continued to favor
approaching Secretary Hull first.

Excerpt from a meeting of the Treasury Department staff, December 18,
1943:[38]

H.M.Jr: Now, the reason of calling you people in is this cable which, I take
it, you have all read.

(Morgenthau was referring to a recent cable from the U.S. Ambassador to Great
Britain, John Winant, to Secretary of State Hull concerning the British government's
view of the licensing request. The ambassador reported that the British opposed the
request because they "are concerned with the difficulties of disposing of any consider-
able number of Jews should they be rescued from enemy occupied territory." Morgen-
thau characterized the British position as "a satanic combination of British chill and
diplomatic double-talk, cold and correct and adding up to a sentence of death."[39])

MR. PEHLE: I think we ought to do some real thinking at this point, Mr. Secretary. As I understand it, the financial thing is out of the way, really, and the British
are saying, in effect, that they don't propose to take any Jews out of those areas.
That is what they say in the first paragraph. They say seventy thousand—they
couldn't—therefore they are not going to go ahead on anything. Now, that is the
general, broad, enormous issue that has been, to some extent, flushed out. . . .

MR. DuBois: Their position is, "What could we do with them if we got
them out?" Amazing, most amazing position.

H.M.Jr: Somebody said they thought that was what was the matter. Was
that your hunch?

MR. PAUL: Luxford said that.

MR. LUXFORD: That is a stock reply when you hit the Jewish problem. . . .

H.M.Jr: Then why don't I ask to see Mr. Hull about this thing Monday?

Mr. DuBois: Mr. Secretary, the only question we have in our mind, I think, is the bull has to be taken by the horns in dealing with this Jewish issue, and get this thing out of the State Department into some agency's hands that is willing to deal with it frontally.

For instance, take the complaint, "What are we going to do with the Jews?"—we let them die because we don't know what to do with them. . . .

Mr. Pehle: It seems to me the only way to get anything done is for the President to appoint a commission or committee consisting of sympathetic people of some importance.

H.M.Jr: But I still think I have got to go to Mr. Hull.

Mr. Pehle: That may be, but I think—

H.M.Jr: Wait a minute, excuse me. I have got to be in a position to say to the President, "Well, I have satisfied myself that Mr. Hull won't go along." I can't say that now. I don't know that Mr. Hull might not go along. . . .

Mr. Luxford: They are not facing up. The issue is very simple for Hull. That is, you can find a million reasons why you can't get them out of Europe, but if somebody put their mind to getting them out, you can then spend the next ten years on what you are going to do with them.

Mr. Paul: Say to the French, "You take them down there."

Mr. Pehle: It has got to be done by somebody who is free to act. But I think you are entirely right that before you go to the President you ought to have Hull's reaction to this cable.

H.M.Jr: I was told last night that the State Department and the Foreign Office are very sensitive to criticism on this Jewish business.

Mr. Luxford: The shoe fits—

H.M.Jr: So, unless you people disagree, I think the thing to do is to exhaust Hull first.

Mr. Paul: I think you ought to.

Mr. DuBois: Because you notice in this very cable they are saying—

H.M.Jr: I would like to say to Mr. Hull, "After all, if you were a member of the Cabinet in Germany today, you would be, most likely, in a prison camp, and your wife would be God knows where," because Mrs. Hull is a Jewess, you know. Did you people know that?

Mr. Luxford: Yes, sir.

H.M.Jr: Her name was Wirtz. And if he was in Germany today, he couldn't hold the position he has, because he is married to a Jewess, even though she changed her name to Whitney. Did you people all know that? (General agreement)[40]

Mr. Paul: I didn't know she changed her name.

H.M.Jr: From Wirtz to Whitney. If I was going from Wirtz, I would have picked up better than Whitney!

Mrs. Klotz:[41] Now you are being very funny. (Laughter) . . .

MR. DuBois: They say they won't let them come out, because if they let a few come out they might get more and wouldn't know what to do with them; therefore they won't let any come out.

MRS. KLOTZ: Tragic!

MR. DuBois: It just speaks for itself—contradicts itself.

* * *

Excerpt from a meeting of the Treasury Department staff, December 19, 1943:[42]

MR. COX: Mr. Secretary, can I pose what your major objective ought to be in terms of the history of this thing, and see what you are shooting at? . . .

H.M.JR: I am listening.

MR. COX: Now, one of your first problems is that [refugees] with a good deal of courage will get out one way or another, or through the underground, and come to a neutral country. What normally happens, what happens in almost all countries under immigration laws, they say, "Do you have any money? Can you support yourself? If you don't have any money, have you got somebody who'll go on bond for you so there are assurances you won't become a public charge?"

The other type of question is through the health authorities, and that is, "How do we know you haven't got typhoid, or what-not?"

The practical fact is that unless you get effective action in all the countries bordering occupied Europe, a good many of these people are turned back, and being turned back means certain death as far as the Germans are concerned. . . .

The first problem, therefore—and you will never get it solved unless the American Government takes a very strong, firm, and persistent position with all the neutral countries where they want to have established places of asylum—is that the people who escape or otherwise get out of the occupied areas can be taken care of in the sense that the neutral country doesn't have to worry about their being charges, that their health is looked after so they don't have to worry about epidemics or contagious diseases, and so forth.

Now, in addition to the strong position of the [U.S.] Government, you need people in those places who are competent, who have got the heart to get this thing done, because the Embassies are not now equipped—or the legations—to handle this problem, which is a very complex and tough problem. . . .

Now, within the State Department there have been basic differences of view on this problem. On the Hill there has been pending before the House Foreign Affairs Committee the so-called Rogers–Gillette resolution to create a special commission to handle this problem. There has been a fight within the House Foreign Affairs Committee on the thing.

Now, my view is that the only way you will solve this thing is if the President, taking yourself, [Undersecretary of State Edward] Stettinius, and [U.S. Custodian of Alien Property Leo] Crowley[43] as the three principal officers of the Government who are concerned directly with the functions that are required to be performed here, and responsible directly to him—not through whatever machinery happens to be in the State Department—to utilize, as far as this group thinks is necessary, in a Governmental Committee—the Africa thing, the Bermuda conference, the private corporations, and so forth; but you need a driving force in this thing that brings the viewpoint before the neutral countries, sees to it that the proper personnel is set up, sees to it there is no defect in the financing, whether the financing is done through the War Contributions Act, through the Lend-Lease Act, and so forth. . . .

The other thing in terms of the President that is basic here, which has come out on the Hill is you also have, incidentally, a domestic political problem, and the people who have been backing the resolution on the Hill are, interestingly enough, with some exceptions all people opposed to the President. . . .

The Secretary of State has never professed to be, and hasn't in fact, been the kind of administrator you are. He just doesn't know a lot of things that are happening inside of the Department until they eventually explode in his face.

On this thing, it has been coasting along; there have been a lot of recommendations written on it, and a lot of testimony up on the Hill. But when you see specific cases like this one, then you realize that the failure of action means that hundreds of thousands of people are being killed.

H.M.Jr: Well, Oscar, I am intrigued by your suggestions, which I think you have told me once before, but a little bit differently, didn't you?

Mr. Cox: Yes, well, we have had a lot of evidence since then, which corroborates the need for it. . . .[44]

Mr. DuBois: You get a committee set up with their heart in it, I feel sure they can do something. . . .

Mr. Luxford: Mr. Secretary, there is a question of marrying these two plans.

H.M.Jr: What two?

Mr. Luxford: We have the specific excuse before us right now for this thing being presented to the President. You will be seeing Mr. Hull tomorrow morning—you are not going to get satisfaction as long as this is left with Long. So you can say, "I think that the two of us should go see the President on this matter right away. It involves the British." . . . [I]f you go to Secretary Hull tomorrow morning and you say, "Now, look, we have to have action," he will say, "I don't know what to do; the British say no." He is going to be very much troubled. You then say, "This looks like a problem the President should have knowledge of. Here are the British taking this dogmatic attitude; let's discuss it with the President. I have a real interest in it." . . . As Mr. DuBois points out, the force is the main issue, because there are no if's and and's in the British position. You can't work out any plan within the terms of their position. They just say, "We don't care how you get them out; we don't know what to do with them." . . . Here is what you have. Oscar has a whale of a good plan, but he has to have an excuse to get it to the President. We have the excuse to get it to the President. We have a beautiful issue here to take to the President and say, "We want a solution to it. The British have taken a dogmatic attitude that we can't solve any of these problems." There is where you marry them.

* * *

On Monday morning, December 20, an elated Morgenthau described to his staff what he regarded as a complete reversal of Hull's position over the course of the weekend and at a meeting earlier that day between Hull, Long, Morgenthau, Pehle, and Paul. But DuBois in particular remained skeptical:[45]

* * *

H.M.Jr: Have you heard the news?

Mr. Luxford: Don't you see us smiling?

Mr. Paul: You fellows register good, because the Secretary didn't think John and I did.

H.M.Jr: Don't worry. This is one of the greatest victories.

Mr. Luxford: It is coming our way.

H.M.Jr: This is one of the most amazing stories since I have been in Washington, it is unbelievable. Around twelve Saturday I phoned Hull's office and found he was home. I made an appointment to see him Monday with regard to this cable from Winant [the U.S. ambassador in London, explaining British opposition to rescue plans]. . . . You fellows don't know old man Hull. He has his teeth in this thing. I have told you fellows consistently not to say a fellow won't come through until the facts are in. The most significant thing he said today was, "The trouble is, the fellows down the line, there are some of them—I don't get a chance to know everything that is going on."

Mr. Pehle: He said, "You just sort of have to rip things out if you want to get them done." . . .

Mr. Luxford: So Hull was worried?

H.M.Jr: Worried! Wait until you hear what he has done! . . .

Mr. Pehle: Before we had had a chance to present the memorandum to Mr. Hull [explaining Treasury's objections to the British and State Department positions], Mr. Hull said that he had focused on the cable from Winant and he had sent a reply. The reply was read and was to the effect that this Government was astounded with the position which the British had taken, and that it was not in accordance with the position of this Government. . . . And that Winant should immediately take the matter up with the British. Mr. Hull indicated that a reply had been received from Winant indicating he was seeing Eden about the matter. . . . At this point, Mr. Hull indicated that some of these matters did not always have his attention, and that he found that it was necessary to go into such matters from top to bottom and avoid people down the line raising technical points, and that in order to get any action it was necessary to "rip" through any objections. . . .

H.M.Jr: . . . And then Long interrupted to say, "Well, I don't know whether you are going to like it or whether you are going to approve or disapprove, but I drafted personally a license Saturday and issued it and cabled it to Switzerland as of last Saturday." . . . [T]he great liberal, Mr. Breckinridge Long, sat down and drafted a license to be issued to Riegner himself, and said he didn't have time or anything else to show it to the Treasury, but he drafted it and ordered Harrison to issue this license to Riegner. . . . [J]ust stop and think. Here, suddenly, out of a clear sky, without consultation with the Treasury, Breckinridge Long on his own issues a license that this thing can be done.

MR. PEHLE: That is right. Long then described—

H.M.JR: I have a couple of cold fish here! (Refers to Mr. Luxford and Mr. DuBois)

MR. LUXFORD: We'll join them in wanting to get to the next step. . . .

H.M.JR: . . . When we came in, before we could say a word, Mr. Hull said to me, in effect—he didn't say it in so many words—"I want to let you know that I have already sent a cable in answer to 8717 from Winant." And he hands me this cable, which was a very powerful cable, which I am to get a copy of. And in that way he took the wind completely out of my sails. . . . [T]he point is that from the time I called the State Department and said that I wanted to have an appointment with Mr. Hull—from that time on something must have happened damned fast. Because Hull must have answered this cable from Winant. I told him in the message what I was going to see him about. He must have gotten hold of Breckinridge Long. Long must have issued a license. When I walked in there Monday morning, the decks were clear. . . . But that is all to the good. It was that telephone call plus this fact that I was coming over, plus this outrageous cable from the British. . . .

MR. LUXFORD: [T]hey saw the record being built up against them.

H.M.JR: It just dynamited this thing loose which has been hanging for five months. I just want to say on the record for you boys—I have said consistently that until I faced Hull on this thing, I wouldn't say that Hull wouldn't do the right thing.

MR. PAUL: We didn't disagree with that.

MR. DUBOIS: We didn't disagree with that. Just as a general statement, I think we all predicted that Long would come through with some very prize statements as to how much he had been doing. My prediction still is to the extent that this is left in the hands of Long and isn't dealt with by Hull that you are not going to have any substantial—

H.M.JR: That is over-obvious.

MR. DUBOIS: I shouldn't have said it!

H.M.JR: No, that's all right.

MR. PAUL: No, it can't be said too often. . . .

H.M.JR:[46] Anyway, boys, thanks to all of you, all of us working together; we have done a job on them.

MR. DUBOIS: This is just the beginning, I am afraid.

H.M.JR: That is all right. You don't know Hull. Now, when Hull has his teeth into this thing, he will not let it go.

MR. PEHLE: Oscar Cox indicated, Mr. Secretary, that the State Department was very, very sensitive about being criticized on this issue. They are being criticized from every front at this point. . . .

H.M.JR: Excuse me just one moment. This is the biggest victory that has happened on this front this year, and I am going to let you couple of old owls sit there and say, "Yes, this is good, but what about tomorrow?" (Laughter)

MR. PEHLE: Maybe they agree with us, Mr. Secretary.

MR. LUXFORD: No, sir, I am very happy.

H.M.JR: We have got Hull on the thing now, and by God, in the face of the [British] Foreign Office they have issued a license. This is what you wanted?

MR. LUXFORD: Exactly. . . .

H.M.JR: . . . But the tragic thing is that—dammit!—this thing might have been done last February. . . .

*   *   *

Although, as noted above, DuBois's primary source of information from within the State Department was Donald Hiss, he also received helpful inside information from Bernard Meltzer,[47] *a lower-level State Department official who, together with his colleague Herbert Feis,*[48] *were lone voices in the department in favor of rescue. At the December 20 meeting, Breckinridge Long tried to blame Meltzer and Feis for the delays in approving the license:*

H.M.JR: . . . Mr. Long took me into another room and said he wanted to talk to me privately.[49] "I just want to tell you," he said, "that unfortunately the people lower down in your Department and lower down in the State Department are making a lot of trouble." He said, "There is a fellow by the name of Meltzer who used to work . . ."

MR. LUXFORD: Meltzer! That is our ally over there!

H.M.JR: Well, he said, "He is the fellow who used to be associated with Feis and he has been spreading this stuff. And he says, "I am storing it up." He spoke about everybody being anti-Semitic and all the rest of that stuff.

As a matter of fact, he said, "Meltzer is one of the fellows who has been raising technical difficulties. I think you ought to know it. I know that he has been creating a lot of trouble."

So I said, "Well, Breck, as long as you raise the question, we might be a little frank. The impression is all around that you, particularly, are anti-Semitic!" I looked him right in the eye. He said, "I know that is so. I hope that you will use your good offices to correct that impression, because I am not." I said, "I am very, very glad to know it." . . . And he protested and said he hoped he could work with me. . . . I said, "After all, Breck, the United States of America was created as a refuge for people who were persecuted the world over, starting with Plymouth."

And I said, "That was the concept of the United States, and as Secretary of Treasury for one hundred and thirty-five million people—I am carrying this out as Secretary of the Treasury, and not as a Jew." So he said, "Well, my concept of

America as a place of refuge for persecuted people is just the same." So I said, "I am delighted to hear that." ...

Is Meltzer no longer with the Department?

MR. DuBois: He is the fellow in the Navy who . . . gave me all this information, how he and Feis were in favor of it and all the rest had opposed it, and how he had tried to fight to put the thing through.

MR. Luxford: Let's say, if you are looking for objective evidence on all that, when Meltzer came over to the Treasury, he was the only State man that argued for it. . . .

H.M.Jr: Don't you fellows feel a little good about this? (To Cox) These fellows are regular icicles over here.

MR. Paul: What do you want us to do?

H.M.Jr: Well, kick up your heels! I once saw Lew Douglas get on that table, roll over on his back, and throw his heels in the air.

MR. Cox: These fellows are more conservative than Lew Douglas. . . .

H.M.Jr: And I don't know whether you will agree with me, that this was the time to bring up this idea of [refugee rescue] committee, because if Hull personally is going to carry the ball and by walking across the street we don't need any committee—

MR. Pehle: Not only that, but that would have been a poor time to raise it.

MR. Cox: I think under the circumstances the committee shouldn't have been raised at this point. . . .

H.M.Jr: Yes, I feel very, very happy, inside, because I was taking an awful risk with the people over there, you know. You didn't know who would take this memorandum, who would take this thing. Supposing Hull was cold on this thing, and didn't want to be bothered—that my memorandum was slipped to Nye or Wheeler or Fish.[50] I realized all of it.

MR. Cox: Sure. You were sticking your neck out. . . .

MR. Luxford: Mr. Secretary, I think that any solemnity that may have been evidenced here is at the next step.

MR. Cox: These fellows give up hard.

MR. Pehle: You see, their issuing a license, Mr. Secretary, doesn't get anybody out of Rumania.

MR. DuBois: We have got to still put—

H.M.Jr: All right, now don't spoil it. I still taste it! I haven't quite digested it. I have seven stomachs like a cow, and I like to ruminate. I am in the process of ruminating now, and chewing my cud until I go through the seventh stomach—not the seventh veil, but the seventh stomach!

*   *   *

Morgenthau at first believed that the State Department's issuing of the license resolved the major issue of dispute between State and Treasury over the refugees. But there was one more issue that was about to explode: the State Department's suppression of news about the mass killings—and its attempt to deceive Morgenthau about its actions. DuBois knew, from the materials that Donald Hiss had shown him, that the State Department's cables revealed its orders to prevent transmission of news about the massacres. At DuBois's suggestion, Morgenthau asked for copies of the relevant cables during the meeting on the morning of December 20. Hull readily agreed and instructed Long to provide them.

At a Treasury meeting that afternoon, Luxford and Pehle reported to Morgenthau on the copies that the State Department had just sent over:

Mr. Luxford: Mr. Secretary, you did not get the cable of January. You didn't even get the reference to it.

Mr. Pehle: They took the reference out.

H.M.Jr: You mean 354 isn't there?

Mr. Luxford: 354 started in the true text: "Your number 4[8]2," so and so, which was deleted in the copy we got. They left out the reference which would have been the cl[ue] to the first cable [482].

H.M.Jr: Which is the first cable?

Mr. Luxford: That was the one which described the conditions [of the Jews who were being persecuted in Europe]. . . .

Mr. White:[51] They were afraid you might tie it in.

*   *   *

Mr. DuBois:[52] So at the [December 20 morning] meeting [with Hull and Long], [Morgenthau] asked if he could be supplied with a copy of this crucial cable—354. So they sent over a copy to him, but they deleted the cross-reference to cable 482. It was an obvious deliberate deception.

Q: What did they take out?

Mr. DuBois: The reference to 482, so all it said was that messages such as those should no longer be sent—it didn't mean anything.

Q: It didn't say what the message was? So the whole substance was gone.

Mr. DuBois: [Morgenthau] once told me—it was some time afterwards—that to him it was the most shocking incident that he had ever experienced during his time in office—the cable of suppression and their deliberate attempt to deceive him with respect to it. . . .

Q: But you had the original cable?

Mr. DuBois: We knew what was in it. So at that point, of course, [Morgenthau] was furious, and he assigned Randolph Paul, then General Counsel of the Treasury Department, to look into the whole matter, and Randolph Paul requested me to look into it, which I did, including a lot of other material.

*   *   *

That same day, Oscar Cox sent Morgenthau drafts of a proposed Executive Order establishing a refugee committee to be cochaired by Hull, Morgenthau, and Crowley and a press release announcing its creation. In his cover letter, Cox remarked that while an executive order was "not necessary," it "might give a stronger foundation to the committee in terms of the necessary power to make it work and in terms of public acceptance." Cox continued: "It might also be that getting the Executive Order signed would forestall some of the action on the Hill in connection with the Rogers–Gillette Resolution."

Receiving no reply from Morgenthau, Cox sent him a note one week later asking if there were anything more he wanted to do about the proposal. The treasury secretary replied on December 31 that "there is nothing that I want to do at the moment concerning the proposed Executive Order or press release on refugees. We are continuing to work on the whole matter here in the Treasury and studying the question very carefully."[53] It would take DuBois's report to finally convince Morgenthau to go further.

IV. The Report

DuBois:[54] [In late December 1943], I prepared that report called "Report to the Secretary on the Acquiescence of This Government in the Murder of the Jews" . . . which not only described this incident of the cable—it described many other things that the State Department was doing with respect to not only suppression of information but their whole attitude toward immigration and the murders of the Jews.

Dorothy DuBois:[55] [H]e wrote it on Christmas day of 1943. Then he told Secretary Morgenthau that we had to give the report to Roosevelt and that if Roosevelt didn't help them [Joe] would resign and tell the papers all about what he found.

The cover note to the memorandum read, in part:

On the basis of the cold facts contained for the most part in State Department documents (which we have finally managed to obtain despite the strenuous opposition of certain State Department officials, including what appears to have been a deliberate falsification of one of the documents) . . . it appears that certain responsible officials of this Government were so fearful that this Government might act to save the Jews of Europe if the gruesome facts relating to Hitler's plans to exterminate them became known, that they not only attempted to suppress the facts but, in addition, they used the powers of their official position to secretly countermand the instructions of the Acting Secretary of State ordering such facts to be reported. We leave it to your judgment whether this action made such officials the accomplices of Hitler in this program and whether or not these officials are not war criminals in every sense of the term.[56]

Notes

1. Richard D. McKinzie interview with Josiah E. DuBois, Jr., Camden, New Jersey, 29 June 1973, Oral History Division, Harry S. Truman Presidential Library.

2. Morgenthau Diaries [hereafter MD], Franklin D. Roosevelt Presidential Library, Hyde Park, NY, 688I/19–20. For more on the experiences of Jews in forced labor camps in North Africa during World War II, see Michel Abitbol, *The Jews of North*

Africa during the Second World War (Detroit: Wayne State University Press, 1989), 150. DuBois's account of his meeting with Wiley would later be cited in discussions about the possible rescue of Jews from Rumania. In an August 1943 memo to Treasury Secretary Morgenthau, DuBois's colleague Randolph Paul argued that "Foreign Service Officers in North Africa" (that is, State Department–appointed diplomats in the region) were a major source of opposition to rescuing the Rumanian Jews because of their fear that those refugees might be evacuated to North Africa, which local Arabs opposed. "In this connection," Paul wrote to Morgenthau, "you may be interested in the attached memorandum prepared by Mr. DuBois while he was in North Africa, after having discussed with Consul General Wiley the question of releasing Jewish refugees from the concentration camps in North Africa." Paul evidently viewed Wiley's statements to DuBois as indicative of the antirefugee mindset among U.S. diplomats abroad. (MD 6881/19–20.)

3. Treasury Department official Edward Bernstein was interviewed by Martin Ostrow for his award-winning PBS documentary, *America and the Holocaust: Deceit and Indifference* (1994). This excerpt is from Ostrow's interview with Bernstein in Washington, D.C., 7 February 1992.

4. John Pehle, Treasury Department official and first director of the War Refugee Board, was interviewed by Martin Ostrow in Bethesda, Maryland, on 2 October 1991. This is an excerpt from that interview.

5. Hillel Kook, better known as Peter Bergson, was the leader of a series of political action committees in the United States during the 1940s that lobbied for rescue of Jews from Hitler and establishment of a Jewish state. This is an excerpt from an interview conducted by M.J. Nurenberger, a veteran Jewish journalist and editor (and himself a Bergson Group activist), in Kfar Shmaryahu, Israel, on 1 July 1971. Transcript in the possession of the author.

6. Morgenthau was related by marriage to the Lehmans, a leading New York banking family of German-Jewish origin. His peers, the brothers Herbert and Irving Lehman, were prominent figures in New York political life; Herbert served as lieutenant governor under Franklin Roosevelt and then as governor (1932–1942); Irving was a justice of the New York State supreme court. They were active in Jewish philanthropies but opposed Zionism and generally argued that Jews should not press President Roosevelt on matters of Jewish concern. Herbert was part of the small group of Jews close to FDR who, as Henry Feingold puts it, "thought of themselves as prominent Americans who incidentally happened to be Jewish . . . [T]hey were not anxious to be overidentified with Jewish causes." Henry L. Feingold, *Bearing Witness: How America and Its Jews Responded to the Holocaust* (Syracuse, NY: Syracuse University Press, 1995), 13.

7. From remarks made by Mr. Morgenthau at "Blowing the Whistle on Genocide: Josiah E. DuBois, Jr., and the Struggle for a U.S. Response to the Holocaust," a conference sponsored by The David S. Wyman Institute for Holocaust Studies at the University of Pennsylvania School of Law, 11 June 2006 (hereafter Wyman Conference). The eldest son of Treasury Secretary Henry Morgenthau, Jr., Henry Morgenthau III is a veteran television and radio producer and writer, most notably with the Boston-based WGBH, which became the flagship producing center for what is now the PBS network. His documentaries won Peabody, Emmy, UPI, and Flaherty Film Festival awards. He has served as a fellow at the Joan Shorenstein Center for Press, Politics, and Public Policy at the Harvard University John F. Kennedy School of Government, and his social history of the Morgenthau family and the world in which they lived,

Mostly Morgenthaus (published by Ticknor and Fields), won the 1992 Jewish Book Council award for best memoir.

8. Robert Morgenthau, son of Henry Morgenthau, Jr., and district attorney of Manhattan, was interviewed by Martin Ostrow in New York City on 29 January 1992. This is an excerpt from that interview.

9. Ostrow interview with Pehle, op. cit.

10. Breckinridge Long (1881–1958), an assistant secretary of state in the Wilson and Roosevelt administrations, assumed responsibility for immigration matters in 1940, and played a central role from 1940 to 1944 in obstructing both Jewish refugee immigration to the United States and rescue initiatives.

11. Ostrow interview with Bernstein, op. cit.

12. Laurence Jarvik interviewed DuBois for his film, *Who Shall Live, Who Shall Die?* (1983), in Camden, NJ, on 23 October 1978. This is an excerpt from that interview.

13. Dr. Gerhart Moritz Riegner (1911–2001), an attorney and native of Berlin, fled the Nazis in 1933 and settled in Switzerland, where he became the Swiss representative of the World Jewish Congress. He later served as secretary general of the World Jewish Congress from 1965 to 1983.

14. Jarvik interview with Gerhart Riegner, New York, NY, undated.

15. The informant was Eduard Schulte (1891–1966), the chief executive officer of a Breslau-based corporation that was Europe's largest producer of zinc, a crucial component in the buildup of the German military. Schulte was secretly opposed to the Nazis. Through his business associate Otto Fitzner, a longtime Nazi Party member with ties to senior party leaders, Schulte obtained inside information about the Hitler regime's plans. When he learned, in July 1942, of the Nazis' plan to murder all of Europe's Jews, he passed the information to a Jewish business colleague of his in Zurich, Isidor Koppelmann. Koppelmann contacted Swiss Jewish journalist Benjamin Sagalowitz, who gave the information to Riegner. Schulte's role in disclosing the information was first made public in Walter Laqueur and Richard Breitman, *Breaking the Silence* (New York: Simon and Schuster, 1986).

16. Stephen S. Wise (1874–1949), a Reform rabbi, was a charismatic orator, outspoken social activist, and the most prominent American Jewish leader during the first half of the twentieth century. He was one of the leaders of the American Zionist movement from its inception in the 1890s and also cofounded the National Association for the Advancement of Colored People (1909) and the American Civil Liberties Union (1920). He founded the American Jewish Congress (1918) and the World Jewish Congress (1936) and chaired the American Zionist Emergency Council during the early 1940s. Wise's early and strong support for Franklin D. Roosevelt and the New Deal earned him greater access to the White House than any other Jewish leader, which increased his stature in the American Jewish community.

17. Sumner Welles (1892–1961) was a veteran Foreign Service officer and State Department official specializing in Latin American affairs. A close personal friend of Franklin D. Roosevelt, Welles in 1933 was chosen by FDR to serve as U.S. ambassador to Cuba, then was later named undersecretary of state (the number two position in the State Department), a post he held from 1937 to 1943.

18. Jarvik interview with DuBois, op. cit.

19. Ostrow interview with Pehle, op. cit.

20. Jarvik interview with DuBois, op. cit.

21. Ray Atherton, acting chief of the State Department's Division of European Affairs.

22. James C. Dunn, an official in the State Department's Division of Political Affairs.

23. Elbridge Durbrow, an official in the State Department's Division of European Affairs.

24. John D. Hickerson, assistant chief of the State Department's Division of European Affairs.

25. Donald Hiss, like his brother Alger, was a State Department official. Alger was at the center of a highly publicized McCarthy-era scandal when he was accused in 1948 of having committed espionage for the Soviet Union. He was convicted of perjury for his statements denying the espionage charge and sentenced to five years in prison.

26. Josiah E. DuBois, Jr., Memorandum for the Files, 18 December 1943, MD 688II/99–100; also see Henry Morgenthau III interview with Josiah E. DuBois, Jr., Pitman, NJ, 26 February 1981, transcript in the possession of the author.

27. Lawrence Glaser interview with Dorothy DuBois, Pittman, NJ, February 2002.

28. MD 688II/99–100.

29. Glaser interview with Dorothy DuBois, op. cit.

30. From remarks made by Mr. Goodwin at the Wyman Conference. Mr. Goodwin, who chaired the conference, has retired from a lengthy and successful career in the home construction business. He is a founder of the National Housing Endowment; the benefactor and also a founder of the Goodwin Holocaust Museum and Education Center of the Delaware Valley, a founder of the National Liberty Museum in Philadelphia, and founder of the Middle East Peace Dialogue Network. His efforts to publicize the heroism of Josiah E. DuBois, Jr., have included creation of a DuBois exhibit in the Holocaust Museum of the Delaware Valley; the establishment of the Josiah DuBois Humanitarian Award; annual gifts to students in the Delaware Valley region whose deeds best exemplify the spirit of DuBois; and the naming of a street in Cherry Hill, New Jersey, after DuBois.

31. Morgenthau interview with DuBois, op. cit.

32. Laurence Jarvik interview with U.S. Rep. Emanuel Celler, New York, NY, 4 October 1978.

33. In 1922, Emanuel Celler (1888–1981) was elected to what would be the first of twenty-five consecutive terms in the U.S. House of Representatives, representing Brooklyn's Tenth District, making him the fourth-longest-serving member in the history of the House. He chaired the House Judiciary Committee for thirteen of his terms. Although a fervent New Dealer and strong supporter of FDR, Celler actively challenged the Roosevelt administration's failure to rescue Jewish refugees.

34. Jarvik interview with DuBois, op. cit.

35. MD 688II/61.

36. "For Sale to Humanity: 70,000 Jews" (advertisement), New York Times, 16 February 1943, 11.

37. Handler to Wyman, 5 March 1985, and Handler to Riegner, 28 July 1992, Milton Handler Papers, Columbia University.

38. MD 688II/82–91.

39. Henry Morgenthau, Jr., "The Morgenthau Diaries VI—The Refugee Run-Around," Colliers, 1 November 1947, 22–23, 62, 65; David S. Wyman, The Abandonment of the Jews: America and the Holocaust, 1941–1945 (New York: Pantheon, 1984), 182.

40. Hull's lack of interest in the plight of European Jewry was due in part to his concern that if he promoted the rescue of refugees critics would ascribe his position to the influence of his wife, Frances Witz (not "Wirtz," as Morgenthau said), whose father was Jewish. Hull, who had presidential ambitions, feared that publicity about his wife's background would harm his electoral chances. FDR encouraged Hull's political aspirations (until Roosevelt decided to run for a third term), but considered Mrs. Hull's Jewish heritage a political liability. The president told Senator Burton Wheeler (D-Montana) in August 1939 that a Hull candidacy would be problematic because Mrs. Hull's ancestry "would be raised" by his opponents. FDR added: "Mrs. Hull is about one quarter Jewish. You and I, Burt, are old English and Dutch stock. We know who our ancestors are. We know there is no Jewish blood in our veins, but a lot of these people do not know whether there is Jewish blood in their veins or not." See "Confidential—Memo on conference at the White House with the President—August 4, 1939," Burton K. Wheeler Papers, Collection 2207, Box 11: File 18, Montana State University, Bozeman, MT.

41. Henrietta Klotz was Secretary Morgenthau's secretary.

42. MD 688II/103–130.

43. Edward Stettinius, Jr. (1900–1949), an executive at U.S. Steel, served the Rooosevelt administration as a director of the U.S. Office of Production Management and then head of the Lend-Lease program. In 1943, he was appointed undersecretary of state, and in November 1944 he succeeded Cordell Hull as secretary of state. He later served as the first U.S. ambassador to the United Nations. Leo T. Crowley (1889–1972) was appointed by President Roosevelt to serve as chairman of the Federal Deposit Insurance Corporation (1934–1943), custodian of alien property (1942–1943), chairman of the Board of Economic Warfare (1943–1944), and chairman of the Foreign Economic Administration (1943–1945).

44. In his remarks in this meeting, Cox also said, "Now, this whole proposition of setting up this Committee has been discussed with the President. He is in favor of it." However, no documents confirming Roosevelt's support for a refugee rescue committee have been located. Cox may have been referring to a statement made by the president in a conversation that was not recorded. In any event, even if FDR did express support for such a committee, there is no evidence he took any steps to bring it to fruition prior to being pressured to do so by Congress and the Treasury Department.

45. MD 688II/148–171.

46. The remaining paragraphs in this section are taken from a Treasury Department staff meeting in January 1944, at which the December 20, 1943, meeting was recalled. See MD 693/79–91.

47. Bernard Meltzer (1914–2007) served at the time as an aide to Assistant Secretary of State Dean Acheson. Later he assisted in drafting the United Nations Charter, and was a prosecutor at the Nuremberg Trials. He taught at the University of Chicago Law School from 1946 to 1985.

48. Herbert Feis (1893–1972) served in the State Department as economic adviser for international affairs. Later he became a prominent historian and won the Pulitzer Prize for History in 1960 for his *Between War and Peace: The Potsdam Conference.*

49. Here the transcript of the December 20 meeting resumes.

50. Congressman Gerald Nye, Senator Burton Wheeler, and Congressman Hamilton Fish were strong opponents of Jewish refugee immigration to the United States.

51. Harry Dexter White (1892–1948) served in the Treasury Department from 1934 to 1947, first as director of monetary research and later as assistant secretary of the treasury.

52. Morgenthau interview with DuBois, op. cit.

53. Cox to Morgenthau, 20 December 1943, MD 688II/191–192; Cox to Morgenthau, 27 December 1943, and Morgenthau to Cox, 31 December 1943, MD 688II/250–251.

54. Morgenthau interview with DuBois, op. cit.

55. Glaser interview with DuBois, op. cit.

56. "Memorandum; for Secretary Morgenthau's Information Only," 23 December 1943, by the Foreign Funds Control Staff, MD 688II/223-J–223-O.

CHAPTER THREE

"The Acquiescence of this Government in the Murder of the Jews"

The full text of the pivotal report to Secretary Morgenthau follows. Authored by Josiah E. DuBois, Jr., the report was initialed by Randolph Paul for the Foreign Funds Control Unit of the Treasury Department. Page numbers of the original document are indicated in brackets.

Jan. 13, 1944

Report to the Secretary on the Acquiescence of this Government in the Murder of the Jews.

One of the greatest crimes in history, the slaughter of the Jewish people in Europe, is continuing unabated.

This Government has for a long time maintained that its policy is to work out programs to save those Jews of Europe who could be saved.

I am convinced on the basis of the information which is available to me that certain officials in our State Department, which is charged with carrying out this policy, have been guilty not only of gross procrastination and wilful failure to act, but even of wilful attempts to prevent action from being taken to rescue Jews from Hitler.

I fully recognize the graveness of this statement and I make it only after having most carefully weighed the shocking facts which have come to my attention during the last several months.

Unless remedial steps of a drastic nature are taken, and taken immediately, I am certain that no effective action will be taken by this Government to prevent the complete extermination of the Jews in German controlled Europe, and that this Government will have to share for all time responsibility for this extermination.

The tragic history of this Government's handling of this matter reveals that certain State Department officials are guilty of the following:

(1) They have not only failed to use the Governmental machinery at their disposal to rescue Jews from Hitler, but have even gone so far as to use this Government machinery to prevent the rescue of these Jews.

(2) They have not only failed to cooperate with private organizations in the efforts of those organizations to work out individual programs of their own, but have taken steps designed to prevent these programs from being put into effect. [1/2]

(3) They not only have failed to facilitate the obtaining of information concerning Hitler's plan to exterminate the Jews of Europe but in their official capacity have gone so far as to surreptitiously attempt to stop the obtaining of information concerning the murder of the Jewish population of Europe.

(4) They have tried to cover up their guilt by:

(a) concealment and misrepresentation;

(b) the giving of false and misleading explanations for their failures to act and their attempts to prevent action; and

(c) the issuance of false and misleading statements concerning the "action" which they have taken to date.

Although only part of the facts relating to the activities of the State Department in this field are available to us, sufficient facts have come to my attention from various sources during the last several months to fully support the conclusions at which I have arrived.

(1) State Department officials have not only failed to use the Governmental machinery at their disposal to rescue the Jews from Hitler, but have even gone so far as to use this Governmental machinery to prevent the rescue of these Jews.

The public record, let alone the facts which have not as yet been made public, reveals the gross procrastination and wilful failure to act of those officials actively representing this Government in this field.

(a) A long time has passed since it became clear that Hitler was determined to carry out a policy of exterminating the Jews in Europe.

(b) Over a year has elapsed since this Government and other members of the United Nations publicly acknowledged and denounced this policy of extermination; and since the President gave assurances that the United States would make every effort together with the United Nations to save those who could be saved. [2/3]

(c) Despite the fact that time is most precious in this matter, State Department officials have been kicking the matter around for over a year without producing results; giving all sorts of excuses for delays upon delays; advancing no specific proposals designed to rescue Jews, at the same time proposing that the whole refugee problem be "explored" by this Government and Intergovernmental Committees. While the State Department has been thus "exploring" the whole refugee problem, without distinguishing between those who are in imminent danger of death and those who are not, hundreds of thousands of Jews have been allowed to perish.

As early as August 1942 a message from the Secretary of the World Jewish Congress in Switzerland (Riegner), transmitted through the British Foreign Office, reported that Hitler had under consideration a plan to exterminate all Jews in German controlled Europe. By November 1942 sufficient evidence had been received, including substantial documentary evidence transmitted through our Legation in Switzerland, to confirm that Hitler had actually adopted and was carrying out his plan to exterminate the Jews. Sumner Welles accordingly authorized the Jewish organizations to make the facts public.

Thereupon, the Jewish organizations took the necessary steps to bring the shocking facts to the attention of the public through mass meetings, etc., and to elicit public support for governmental action. On December 17, 1942, a joint statement of the United States and the European members of the United Nations was issued calling attention to and denouncing the fact that Hitler was carrying into effect his oft-repeated intention to exterminate the Jewish people in Europe.

Since the time when this Government knew that the Jews were being murdered, our State Department has failed to take any positive steps reasonably calculated to save any of these people. Although State has used the devices of setting up inter-governmental organizations to survey the whole refugee problem, and calling conferences such as the Bermuda Conference to explore the whole refugee problem, making it appear that positive action could be expected, in fact nothing has been accomplished.
[3/4]

Before the outcome of the Bermuda conference, which was held in April 1943, was made public, Senator Langer prophetically stated in an address in the Senate on October 6, 1943:

"As yet we have had no report from the Bermuda Refugee Conference. With the best good will in the world and with all latitude that could and should be accorded to diplomatic negotiations in time of war, I may be permitted to voice the bitter suspicion that the absence of a report indicates only one thing—the lack of action.

"Probably in all 5703 years, Jews have hardly had a time as tragic and hopeless as the one which they are undergoing now. One of the most tragic factors about the situation is that while singled out for suffering and martyrdom by their enemies, they seem to have been forgotten by the nations which claim to fight for the cause of humanity. We should remember the Jewish slaughterhouse of Europe and ask what is being done—and I emphasize the word 'done'—to get some of these suffering human beings out of the slaughter while yet alive.

" * * * Perhaps it would be necessary to introduce a formal resolution or to ask the Secretary of State to report to an appropriate congressional committee on the steps being taken in this connection. Normally it would have been the job of the Government to show itself alert to this tragedy; but when a government neglects a duty it is the job of the legislature in a democracy to remind it of that duty. * * * It is not important who voices a call for action, and it is not important what procedure is being used in order to get action. It is important that action be undertaken."

Similar fears were voiced by <u>Representatives Celler, Dickstein, and Klein.</u> <u>Senator Wagner and Representative Sadowski</u> also issued calls for <u>action</u>.

The widespread fears concerning the failure of the Bermuda Conference were fully confirmed when Breckinridge Long finally revealed some of the things that had happened at that Conference in his statement before the Committee on Foreign Affairs of the House on November 26, 1943.

After Long's "disclosure" <u>Representative Celler</u> stated in the House on December 20, 1943:

[4/5]

"He discloses some of the things that happened at the so-called Bermuda Conference. He thought he was telling us something heretofore unknown and secret. What happened at the Bermuda Conference could not be kept executive. All the recommendations and findings of the Bermuda Conference were made known to the Intergovernmental Committee on Refugees in existence since the Evian Conference on Refugees in 1938 and which has been functioning all this time in London. How much has that committee accomplished in the years of its being. It will be remembered that the Intergovernmental Committee functions through an executive committee composed of six countries, the United States, the United Kingdoms, the Netherlands, France, Brazil, and Argentina. True, no report of the Bermuda Conference was made public. But a strangely ironical fact will be noted in the presence of Argentina on this most trusted of committees, Argentina that provoked the official reprimand of President Roosevelt by its banning of the Jewish Press, and within whose borders Nazi propagandists and falangists now enjoy a Roman holiday. I contend that by the very nature of its composition the Intergovernmental Committee on Refugees cannot function successfully as the instrumentality to rescue the Jewish people of Europe. The benefits to be d[e]rived from the Bermuda Conference like those of the previous Evian Conference can fit into a tiny capsule."

One of the best summaries of the whole situation is contained in one sentence of a report submitted on December 30, 1943, by the Committee on Foreign Relations of the Senate, recommending the passage of a Resolution (S.R.203) favoring the appointment of a commission to formulate plans to save the Jews of Europe from extinction by Nazi Germany. The Committee stated:

<u>"We have talked; we have sympathized; we have expressed our horror; the</u> <u>time to act is long past due."</u>

The Senate Resolution had been introduced by Senator Guy M. Gillette in behalf of himself and eleven colleagues, Senators Taft, Thomas, Radcliffe, Murray, Johnson, Guffey, Ferguson, Clark, Van Nuys, Downey, and Ellender.

The House Resolutions (H.R.'s 350 and 352), identical with the Senate Resolution, were introduced by Representatives Baldwin and Rogers.

[5/6]

The most glaring example of the use of the machinery of this Government to actually prevent the rescue of Jews is the administrative restrictions which have been placed upon the granting of visas to the United States. In the note which the State Department sent to the British on February 26, 1943 it was stated:

"Since the entry of the United States into the war there have been no new restrictions placed by the Government of the United States upon the number of aliens of any nationality permitted to proceed to this country under existing laws, except for the more intensive examination of aliens required for security reasons." (Underscoring supplied)

The exception for "security reasons" mentioned in this note is the joker. Under the pretext of security reasons so many difficulties have been placed in the way of refugees obtaining visas that it is no wonder that the admission of refugees to this country does not come anywhere near the quota, despite Long's statement designed to create the impression to the contrary. The following administrative restrictions which have been applied to the issuance of visas since the beginning of the war are typical.

(a) Many applications for visas have been denied on the grounds that the applicants have close relatives in Axis controlled Europe. The theory of this is that the enemy would be able to put pressure on the applicant as a result of the fact that the enemy has the power of life or death over his immediate family.

(b) Another restriction greatly increases the red tape and delay involved in getting the visa and requires among other things two affidavits of support and sponsorship to be furnished with each application for a visa. To each affidavit of support and sponsorship there must be attached two letters of reference from two reputable American citizens.

[6/7]

If anyone were to attempt to work out a set of restrictions specifically designed to prevent Jewish refugees from entering this country it is difficult to conceive of how more effective restrictions could have been imposed than have already been imposed on grounds of "security".

It is obvious of course that these restrictions are not essential for security reasons. Thus refugees upon arriving in this country could be placed in interment camps similar to those used for the Japanese on the West Coast and released only after a satisfactory investigation. Furthermore, even if we took these refugees and treated them as prisoners of war it would be better than letting them die.

Representative Dickstein stated in the House on December 15:

"If we consider the fact that the average admission would then be at the rate of less than 58,000 per year, it is clear that the organs of our Government have not done their duty. The existing quotas call for the admission of more than 150,000 every year, so that if the quotas themselves had been filled there would have been a total of one-half million and not 580,000 during the period mentioned.

"But that is not the whole story. There was no effort of any kind made to save from death many of the refugees who could have been saved during the time that transportation lines were available and there was no obstacle to their admission to the United States. But the obstructive policy of our organs of Government, particularly the State Department, which saw fit to hedge itself about with rules and regulations, instead of lifting rules and regulations, brought about a condition so that not even the existing immigration quotas are filled."

Representative Celler stated in the House on June 30:

"Mr. Speaker, nations have declared war on Germany, and their high-ranking officials have issued pious protestations against the [7/8] Nazi massacre of Jewish victims, but not one of those countries thus far has said they would be willing to accept these refugees either permanently or as visitors, or any of the minority peoples trying to escape the Hitler prison and slaughterhouse.

"Goebbels says: 'The United Nations won't take any Jews. We don't want them. Let's kill them.' And so he and Hitler are making Europe Judentun.

"Without any change in our immigration statutes we could receive a reasonable number of those who are fortunate enough to escape the Nazi hellhole, receive them as visitors, the immigration quotas notwithstanding. They could be placed in camps or cantonments and held there in such havens until after the war. Private charitable agencies would be willing to pay the entire cost thereof. They would be no expense to the Government whatsoever. These agencies would even pay for transportation by ships to and from this country.

"We house and maintain Nazi prisoners, many of them undoubtedly responsible for Nazi atrocities. We should do no less for the victims of the rage of the Huns."

Again, on December 20, he stated:

"According to Earl G. Harrison, Commissioner of the Immigration and Naturalization Service, not since 1862 have there been fewer aliens entering the country.

"Frankly, Breckinridge Long, in my humble opinion, is least sympathetic to refugees in all the State Department. I attribute to him the tragic bottleneck in the granting of visas.

"The Interdepartmental Review Committees which review the applications for visas are composed of one official, respectively, from each of the following Departments: War, Navy, F.B.I., State, and Immigration. That committee has been glacierlike in its slowness and coldbloodedness. It take[s] months and months to grant the visas and then it usually applies to a corpse.

"I brought this difficulty to the attention of the President. He asked Long to investigate at once. No, there has been no change in conditions. The gruesome bottleneck still exists."

[8/9]

(2) State Department officials have not only failed to cooperate with private organizations in the efforts of these organizations to work out individual programs of their own, but have taken steps designed to prevent these programs from being put into effect.

The best evidence in support of this charge are the facts relating to the proposal of the World Jewish Congress to evacuate thousands of Jews from Rumania and France. The highlights relating to the efforts of State Department officials to prevent this proposal from being put into effect are the following:

(a) On March 13, 1943, a cable was received from the World Jewish Congress representative in London stating that information reaching London indicated the possibility of rescuing Jews provided funds were put at the disposal of the World Jewish Congress representation in Switzerland.

(b) On April 10, 1943, Sumner Welles cabled our Legation in Bern and requested them to get in touch with the World Jewish Congress representative in Switzerland, whom Welles had been informed was in possession of important information regarding the situation of the Jews.

(c) On April 20, 1943, a cable was received from Bern relating to the proposed financial arrangements in connection with the evacuation of the Jews from Rumania and France.

(d) On May 25, 1943, State Department cabled for a clarification of these proposed financial arrangements. This matter was not called to the attention of the Treasury Department at this time.

(e) This whole question of financing the evacuation of the Jews from Rumania and France was first called to the attention of the Treasury Department on June 25, 1943.

(f) A conference was held with the State Department relating to this matter on July 15, 1943.

(g) One day after this conference, on July 16, 1943, the Treasury Department advised the State Department that it was prepared to issue a license in this matter.

(h) The license was not issued until December 18, 1943.

[9/10]

During this five months period between the time that the Treasury stated that it was prepared to issue a license and the time when the license was actually issued delays and objections of all sorts were forthcoming from officials in the State Department, our Legation in Bern, and finally the British. The real significance of these delays and objections was brought home to the State Department in letters which you sent to Secretary Hull on November 24, 1943, and December 17, 1943, which completely devastated the "excuses" which State Department officials had been advancing. On December 10 you made an appointment to discuss the matter with Secretary Hull on December 20. And then an amazing but under-standable thing happened. On December 13, the day after you sent your letter and the day on which you requested an appointment with Secretary Hull, the State Department sent a telegram to the British Foreign Office expressing astonishment with the British point of view and stating that the Department was unable to agree with that point of view (in simple terms, the British point of view referred to by the State Department is that they are apparently prepared to accept the pos-sible—even probable—death of thousands of Jews in enemy territory because of "the difficulties of disposing of any considerable number of Jews should they be rescued"). On the same day, the State Department issued a license notwithstand-ing the fact that the objections of our Legation in Bern were still outstanding and that British disapproval had already been expressed. State Department officials were in such a hurry to issue this license that they not only did not ask the Trea-sury to draft the license (which would have been the normal procedure) but they drafted the license themselves and issued it without even consulting the Treasury as to its terms. Informal discussions with certain State Department officials have confirmed what is obvious from the above mentioned facts.

Breckinridge Long knew that his position was so indefensible that he was unwilling to even try to defend it at your pending conference with Secretary Hull on December 20. Accordingly, he took such action as he felt was necessary to "cover up" his previous position in this matter. It is, of course, clear that if we had not made the record against the State Department followed by your request to see Secretary Hull, the action which the State Department officials took on De-cember 10 would either never have been taken at all or would have been delayed so long that any benefits which it might have had would have been lost. [10/11]

(3) State Department officials not only have failed to facilitate the obtain-ing of information concerning Hitler's plans to exterminate the Jews of Europe but in their official capacity have gone so far as to surreptitiously attempt to stop the obtaining of information concerning the murder of the Jewish population in Europe.

The evidence supporting this conclusion is so shocking and so tragic that it is difficult to believe.

The facts are as follows:

(a) Sumner Welles as Acting Secretary of State requests confirmation of Hitler's plan to exterminate the Jews. Having already received various reports on the plight of the Jews, on October 5, 1942 Sumner Welles as Acting Secre-tary of State sent a cable (2314) for the personal attention of Minister Harrison in Bern stating that leaders of the Jewish Congress had received reports from their representatives in Geneva and London to the effect that many thousands of Jews in Eastern Europe were being slaughtered pursuant to a policy embarked upon by the German Government for the complete extermination of the Jews in Europe. Welles added that he was trying to obtain further information from the

Vatican but that other than this he was unable to secure [10/11] confirmation of these stories. We stated that Rabbi Wise believed that information was available to his representatives in Switzerland but that they were in all likelihood fearful of dispatching any such reports through open cables or mail. He then stated that Riegner and Lichtheim were being requested by Wise to call upon Minister Harrison; and Welles requested Minister Harrison to advise him by telegram of all the evidence and facts which he might secure as a result of conferences with Riegner and Lichtheim.

(b) State Department receives confirmation and shocking evidence that extermination was being rapidly and effectively carried out. Pursuant to Welles' cable of October 5 Minister Harrison forwarded documents from Riegner confirming the fact of extermination of the Jews (in November 1942), and in a cable of January 21, 1943 (482) relayed a message from Riegner and Lichtheim which Harrison stated was for the information of the Under Secretary of State (and was to be transmitted to Rabbi Stephen Wise if the Under Secretary should so determine). This message described a horrible situation concerning the plight of the Jews in Europe. It reported mass [11/12] executions of Jews in Poland; according to one source 6,000 Jews were being killed daily; the Jews were required before execution to strip themselves of all their clothing which was then sent to Germany; the remaining Jews in Poland were confined to ghettos, etc.; in Germany deportations were continuing; many Jews were in hiding and there had been many cases of suicide; Jews were being deprived of rationed foodstuffs; no Jews would be left in Prague or Berlin by the end of March, etc.; and in Rumania 130,000 Jews were deported to Transnistria; about 60,000 had already died and the remaining 70,000 were starving; living conditions were indescribable; Jews were deprived of all their money, foodstuffs and possessions; they were housed in deserted cellars, and occasionally twenty to thirty people slept on the floor of one unheated room; disease was prevalent, particularly fever; urgent assistance was needed.

(c) Sumner Welles furnishes this information to the Jewish organizations. Sumner Welles furnished the documents received in November to the Jewish organizations in the United States and authorized them to make the facts public. On February 9, 1943 Welles forwarded the horrible message contained in cable 432 of January 21 to Rabbi Stephen Wise. In his letter of February 9 Welles stated that he was pleased to be of assistance in this matter.

Immediately upon the receipt of this message, the Jewish organizations arranged for a public mass meeting in Madison Square Garden in a further effort to obtain effective action.

(d) Certain State Department officials surreptitiously attempt to stop this Government from obtaining further information from the very source from which the above evidence was received. On February 10, the day after Welles forwarded the message contained in cable 482 of January 21 to Rabbi Wise, and in direct response to this cable, a most highly significant cable was dispatched. This cable, 354 of February 10, read as follows:

"Your 432, January 21

"In the future we would suggest that you do not accept reports submitted to you to be transmitted to private persons in the United States unless such action is advisable because of extraordinary circumstances. Such private messages circumvent neutral countries' censorship and it is felt that by sending them [12/13] we risk the possibility that steps would necessarily be taken by the neutral countries to curtail or forbid our means of communication for confidential official matter.

Hull (SW)"

Although this cable on its face is most innocent and innocuous, when read together with the previous cables I am forced to conclude it is nothing less than an attempted suppression of information requested by this Government concerning the murder of Jews by Hitler.

Although this cable was signed for Hull by "SW" (Sumner Welles) it is significant that there is not a word in the cable that would even suggest to the person signing it that it was designed to countermand the Department's specific requests for information on Hitler's plans to exterminate the Jews. The cable appeared to be a normal routine message which a busy official would sign without question.

I have been informed that the initialled file copy of the cable bears the initials of Atherton and Dunn as well as of Durbrow and Hickerson.

(c) Thereafter Sumner Welles again requested our legation on April 19, 1943 (cable 877) for information, apparently not realizing that in cable 354 (to which he did not refer) Harrison had been instructed to cease forwarding reports of this character. Harrison replied on April 20 (cable 2460) and indicated that he was in a most confused state of mind as a result of the conflicting instructions he had received. Among other things he stated: "May I suggest that messages of this character should not (repeat not) be subjected to the restriction imposed by your 354, February 10, and that I be permitted to transmit messages from R more particularly in view of the helpful information which they may frequently contain?"

The fact that cable 354 is not the innocent and routine cable that it appears to be on its face is further highlighted by the efforts of State Department officials to prevent this Department from obtaining the cable and learning its true significance.

[13/14]

The facts relating to this attempted concealment are as follows:

(i) Several men in our Department had requested State Department officials for a copy of the cable of February 10 (354). We had been advised that it was a Department communication; a strictly political communication, which had nothing to do with economic matters; that it had only had a very limited distribution within the Department, the only ones having anything to do with it being the European Division, the Political Adviser and Sumner Welles; and that a copy could not be furnished to the Treasury.

(ii) At the conference in Secretary Hull's office on December 20 in the presence of Breckinridge Long, you asked Secretary Hull for a copy of cable 354, which you were told would be furnished to you.

(iii) By note to you of December 20, Breckinridge Long enclosed a paraphrase of cable 354. This paraphrase of cable 354 specifically <u>omitted any reference to cable 482 of January 21</u>—thus destroying the only tangible clue to the true meaning of the message.

(iv) You would never have learned the true meaning of cable 354 had it not been for the fact that one of the men in my office whom I had asked to obtain all the facts on this matter for me had previously called one of the men in another Division of the State Department and requested permission to see the cable. In view of the Treasury interest in this matter this State Department representative obtained cable 354 and the cable of January 21 to which it referred and showed these cables to my man.

(4) <u>The State Department officials have tried to cover up their guilt by:</u>

(a) <u>concealment and misrepresentation</u>

In addition to concealing the true facts from and misrepresenting these facts to the public, State Department officials have even attempted concealment and misrepresentation within the Government. The most striking example of this is [14/15] the above mentioned action taken by State Department officials to prevent this Department from obtaining a copy of cable 354 of February 10 (which stopped the obtaining of information concerning the murder of Jews); and the fact that after you had requested a copy of this cable, State Department officials forwarded the cable to us with its most significant part omitted, thus destroying the whole meaning of the cable.

(b) <u>the giving of false and misleading explanations for their failures to act and their attempts to prevent action.</u>

The outstanding explanation of a false and misleading nature which the State Department officials have given for their failures to work out programs to rescue Jews, and their attempts to prevent action, are the following:

(i) The nice sounding but vicious theory that the whole refugee problem must be explored and consideration given to working out programs for the relief of *all* refugees whose lives are in imminent danger and those whose lives are not in imminent danger.

(ii) The argument that various proposals cannot be acted upon promptly by this Government but must be submitted to the Executive Committee of the Intergovernmental Committee on Refugees. This Committee has taken no effective action to actually evacuate refugees from enemy territory and it is at least open to doubt whether it has the necessary authority to deal with the matter.

(iii) The argument that the extreme restrictions which the State Department has placed on the granting of visas to refugees is necessary for "security reasons." The falsity of this argument has already been dealt with in this memorandum.

The false and misleading explanations, which the State Department officials gave for delaying for over six months the program of the World Jewish Congress for the evacuation of thousands of Jews from Rumania and France, are dealt with in your letter to Secretary Hull of December 17, 1943.
[15/16]

A striking example is the argument of the State Department officials that the proposed financial arrangement might benefit the enemy. It is of course not surprising that the same State Department officials who usually argue that economic warfare considerations are not important should in this particular case attempt to rely on economic warfare considerations to kill the proposed program.

In this particular case, the State Department officials attempted to argue that the relief plan might benefit the enemy by facilitating the acquisition of funds by the enemy. In addition to the fact that this contention had no merit whatsoever by virtue of the conditions under which the local funds were to be acquired, it is significant that this consideration had not been regarded as controlling in the past by the State Department officials, even where no such conditions had been imposed.

Thus, in cases involving the purchase, by branches of United States' concerns in Switzerland, of substantial amounts of material in enemy territory, State Department officials have argued that in view of the generous credit supplied by the Swiss to the Germans "transactions of this type cannot be regarded as actually increasing the enemy's purchasing power in Switzerland which is already believed to be at a maximum". It is only when these State Department officials really desire to prevent a transaction that they advance economic warfare considerations as a bar.

(c) the issuance of false and misleading statements concerning the "action" which they have taken to date.

It is unnecessary to go beyond Long's testimony to find many examples of misstatements. His general pious remarks concerning what this Government has done for the Jews of Europe; his statement concerning the powers and functions of the Intergovernmental Committee on Refugees; his reference to the "screening process" set up to insure wartime security, etc., have already been publicly criticized as misrepresentations.

A statement which is typical of the way Long twists facts is his remarks concerning the plan of a Jewish agency to send money to Switzerland to be used through the International Red Cross to buy food to take care of Jews in parts of Czechoslovakia and Poland. Long indicates that the Jewish agency requested that [16/17] the money be sent through the instrumentality of the Intergovernmental Committee. I am informed that the Jewish agency wished to send the money immediately to the International Red Cross and it was Long who took the position that the matter would have to go through the Intergovernmental Committee, thereby delaying the matter indefinitely. Long speaks of an application having been filed with the Treasury to send some of this money and that the State

Department was supporting this application to the Treasury. The facts are that no application has ever been filed with the Treasury and the State Department has at no time indicated to the Treasury that it would support any such application.

The most patent instance of a false and misleading statement is that part of Breckinridge Long's testimony before the Committee on Foreign Affairs of the House (November 26, 1943) relating to the admittance of refugees into this country. Thus, he stated:

" * * * We have taken into this country since the beginning of the Hitler regime and the persecution of the Jews, until today, approximately 580,000 refugees. The whole thing has been under the quota, during the period of 10 years —all under the quota—except the generous gesture we made with visitors' and transit visas during an awful period."

Congressman Emanuel Celler in commenting upon Long's statement in the House on December 20, 1943, stated:

" * * * In the first place these 580,000 refugees were in the main ordinary quota immigrants coming in from all countries. The majority were not Jews. His statement drips with sympathy for the persecuted Jews, but the tears he sheds are crocodile. I would like to ask him how many Jews were admitted during the last 3 years in comparison with the number seeking entrance to preserve life and dignity. * * * One gets the impression from Long's statement that the United States has gone out of its way to help refugees fleeing death at the hands of the Nazis. I deny this. On the contrary, the State Department has turned its back on the time-honored principle of granting havens to refugees. The tempest-tossed get little comfort from men like Breckinridge Long. * * * Long says [17/18] that the door to the oppressed is open but that it 'has been carefully screened.' What he should have said is 'barlocked and bolted.' By the act of 1924, we are permitted to admit approximately 150,000 immigrants each year. During the last fiscal year only 23,725 came as immigrants. Of these only 4, 705 were Jews fleeing Nazi persecution.

* * *

"If men of the temperament and philosophy of Long continue in control of immigration administration, we may as well take down that plaque from the Statue of Liberty and black out the 'lamp beside the golden door.'"

RP

CHAPTER FOUR

Confronting the President

The title of DuBois's report, "Report to the Secretary on the Acquiescence of this Government in the Murder of the Jews," left no doubt that the contents were political dynamite. But DuBois knew the report would have an impact only if Morgenthau were prepared to use it. The treasury secretary was reluctant to approach President Roosevelt on the rescue issue, preferring to go through the regular channels, that is, the State Department. Hoping to force Morgenthau's hand, DuBois decided to up the ante.

* * *

DuBois:[1] I had the feeling from a few things that [Secretary Morgenthau] had said that Roosevelt was not the greatest—let's put it this way—on this Jewish problem. So after the report was prepared, which [Morgenthau] was going to deliver to Roosevelt . . . I said, Mr. Secretary, if it means anything and if you want to, you can tell the President—if the President doesn't take any action on this report, I'm going to resign and release the report to the press. Whether he ever told that to Roosevelt or not, I don't know, probably not, but I just don't know. That's how deep I felt about the thing, and I think that also impressed [Morgenthau], the fact that I was willing to resign. I would have to. Believe me, I would have, if the President hadn't acted. . . . I have a feeling [Morgenthau] acted because he knew if he didn't act, it was going to become a very explosive thing politically. And that's why he acted, would be my guess.

Joan Morgenthau:[2] My father's relationship with the President was a very close and very intense relationship. Over a period of many, many years. And I do think it was one of the most important things to him in his life. And it was not a—it was not always an easy relationship. My father used to say that he was, he was the favorite whipping boy. And he used that term quite often when things, when things didn't go well. . . . [M]y father didn't want to push things too far. And for example, I think that as a Jew he felt that he needed almost to be extra careful to be sure that he was speaking first as an American and only secondly as a Jew. And although he was sensitized to kinds of issues that people perhaps who were not Jewish were not very sensitive to at that time, he didn't want to push it as a Jew. He wanted to make it very clear that he felt that he was, there was no doubt that he was an American. . . . I think it must have been very difficult for him to—to push the issue to the extent that he did when he felt that he just had to go circumvent the State Department at any cost. I think that must have been difficult. I think he felt that he was pushing the boundaries of his, of his relationship. But I think he felt by that time so strongly that something had to be done that he was willing to take that chance.

PEHLE:[3] [It] was a strong report to Morgenthau, stating in the starkest terms what had happened, that we had caught the State Department suppressing information. We had caught them trying to cover it up and that action had to be taken. . . . The Secretary agreed that he should go to see the President, but he first asked us to write another memorandum based on the first one, from himself to the President. Which we did. . . . The memorandum we prepared from the Secretary to the President was in more moderate tones but still insisted that action had to be taken right away. The Secretary knew that he had to act. And he arranged an appointment with the President Sunday afternoon, which was not ordinarily the time for business at the White House.

It was not an easy thing for [Morgenthau] to do because he did not want to be the spokesman for Jewish interests. But on the other hand, he knew that he had to use his relationship with the President in this particular area.

DuBois:[4] [The] report . . . said, "the tragic history of this government's handling of this matter—namely the slaughter of the Jewish people in Europe—reveals that certain State Department officials are guilty of the following: one, they have not only failed to use the governmental machinery at their disposal to rescue Jews from Hitler, but have gone so far as to use this governmental machinery to prevent the rescue of these Jews. And secondly, they have not only failed to cooperate with private organizations in the efforts of these organizations to work out individual programs of their own, but they have taken steps designed to prevent these programs from being put into effect. Third, they not only have failed to facilitate the obtaining of information concerning Hitler's plans to exterminate the Jews of Europe, but in their official capacity, have gone so far as to surreptitiously attempt to stop the obtaining of information concerning the murder of the Jewish people of Europe."

And then we charge that they have tried to cover up their guilt by concealment and misrepresentation, the giving of false and misleading explanations, and issuance of false and misleading statements. The third point that we made, namely their attempt to prevent information from being made available to the American people about the murder of the Jews, I think is one of the most shocking stories—not stories—shocking series of events, that has ever come to my attention during the ten years of government service.

And I know that Secretary Morgenthau, not too long before he died, told me that it is the most shocking thing that had ever come to his attention during the time that he was in government service. . . .

The report was reviewed by John Pehle who toned down some of my rather—unusually strong language, but he kept most of it in there, and it was signed by Randolph Paul and was presented to the Secretary of the Treasury, who presented it to President Roosevelt in a shortened form. . . . And that led directly to the creation of the War Refugee Board.

* * *

Excerpts from a meeting of the Treasury Department staff, January 13, 1944:[5]

MR. PAUL: I think it might be helpful if you would go over this written report before we have a meeting. . . .

(Mr. Paul hands the Secretary an eighteen-page intradepartmental Memorandum of January 13, 1944.)

MR. DUBOIS: This is just to the Secretary.

MR. PAUL: This is in the Department, here. It is intended as a report to you. It is not an outside document.

H.M.JR: It has got a nice title, anyway. . . . Now, in the meantime, what do I do?

MR. PAUL: We had anticipated having ready for you Monday a report from you which goes out of the Department; that is, goes to the President.

* * *

Pehle then read from a document in which the U.S. commanding general of North African theater operations rejected suggestions that American forces evacuate three thousand Yugoslav Jews stranded on the island of Rab, near Italy, which was in danger of being reoccupied by the Germans. Among the reasons the general cited was that "to take such action might create a precedent which would lead to other demands and an influx of additional refugees."

* * *

H.M.JR: Gentlemen, may I say this? What the Commanding General says is no different from what the English Foreign Office says, and what everybody else has said. The whole strain is this: "This thing is a damned nuisance."

MR. DUBOIS: That is it.

MR. LUXFORD: "Why would we be tagged with it?" That is what he says.

H.M.JR: When you get through with it, the attitude to date is no different from Hitler's attitude.

MRS. KLOTZ: Exactly.

MR. WHITE: I think it is worse, because it is covered up by a species of hypocrisy in which men are deterred from doing what they should wish to do, either because it is difficult—

MR. GASTON:[6] You are unfair. We don't shoot them. We let other people shoot them, and let them starve.

Mr. Paul: Starve and get all kinds of diseases.

Mr. White: It is curious how many different reasons can be thought up for not taking action.

Mr. Paul: Haven't got any water—haven't got any ships.

Mr. White: Yes, didn't have any water down in North Africa.

Mr. Paul: How the devil a lot of these people lived there before, I don't know. . . .

H.M.Jr: . . . Supposing I go to the President with the most terrific document of condemnation of these people, and he turns to me and says, "Henry, I have never been so shocked in my life. What can I do?"

Mr. White: We have a specific proposal.

Mr. Pehle: An Executive Order, Mr. Secretary.

Mr. Paul: You won't have to go to him with no implementation.

H.M.Jr: But the thing is even more shocking because, I think, in some of these cases that I have listened to, the time has gone by that you can do anything.

Mr. Pehle: That is where we don't hear about them until it is too late.

Mr. Gaston: This commanding general's document there is tremendously shocking to me, because what he says is, "We don't want to give any physical or monetary aid to these people on this island because it will create a precedent and stimulate an influx of refugees, and we are not ready and don't want to take care of them."

* * *

Meanwhile, the rescue issue had become the focus of a steadily escalating conflict in Congress, thanks to the introduction, in November 1943, of the aforementioned Gillette-Rogers resolution, which the Bergson Group had drafted. The resolution stated:

Whereas the Congress of the United States, by concurrent resolution adopted on March 15 of this year, expressed its condemnation of Nazi Germany's "mass murder of Jewish men, women, and children," a mass crime which has already exterminated close to two million human beings, about 30 percentum of the total Jewish population of Europe, and which is growing in intensity as Germany approaches defeat;

Whereas the American tradition of justice and humanity dictates that all possible means be employed to save from this fate the surviving Jews of Europe, some four million souls who have been rendered homeless and destitute by the Nazis: Therefore be it

Resolved, That the House of Representatives recommends and urges the creation by the President of a commission of diplomatic, economic, and military experts to formulate and effectuate a plan of immediate action designed to save the surviving Jewish people of Europe from extinction at the hands of Nazi Germany.[7]

* * *

U.S. Rep. Sol Boom (D-New York), chairman of the House Committee on Foreign Affairs and a strong supporter of the administration's refugee policy, attempted to undermine the resolution by insisting on holding full hearings. Bloom had served as a U.S. delegate to the sham refugee conference in Bermuda and was stung by the Bergson-led criticism of his role there. Congressional hearings are ordinarily held only to consider items of legislation, whereas the rescue resolution was merely a nonbinding Congressional recommendation. Nonetheless, at Bloom's direction, hearings on the Gillette–Rogers resolution got underway on November 19, 1943. Witnesses supporting the resolution included Bergson Group activist and American Labor Party leader Dean Alfange, publisher William Ziff, and Bergson himself. As the hearings continued into the following week, the committee heard from additional supporters of the resolution, such as New York City Mayor Fiorello La Guardia, author Frances Gunther, and Lewis Hines, assistant to the president of the American Federation of Labor.[8]

Hillel Kook (Peter Bergson), in 1948.

Two witnesses testified against the resolution. One was Rabbi Dr. Stephen Wise, who took part in the hearings in his capacity as chairman of the American Jewish Conference, a coalition of mainstream Jewish organizations. Wise testified that "of course we favor" the resolution but then criticized it as "inadequate" and urged that it be amended to mention Palestine as a destination for Jewish refugees.[9] *Bergson, like Wise, strongly favored Jewish immigration to Palestine, but he had deliberately omitted Palestine from the resolution in order to avoid antagonizing members of Congress who would not support implicit criticism of Great Britain, America's ally. Wise's position on the rescue resolution may have also reflected his antagonism in general toward the Bergson Group, which was rooted in concern that Bergson was usurping the established Jewish leadership in the eyes of the public, media, and government officials.*

The other witness to testify against the resolution was Assistant Secretary of State Breckinridge Long.

* * *

Excerpts from the testimony of Breckinridge Long before the House Committee on Foreign Affairs, November 26, 1943:

LONG: . . . [T]he historic attitude of the United States as a haven for the oppressed has not been stopped. The Department of State has kept the door open. It is carefully screened, but the door is open. . . . Something over a year ago a delegation of some of the Jewish leaders talked to me, and they thought that it would be far better if there could be, instead of one government being active, other governments taking part in this activity. Of course, we had no desire to inject any difference of thought in the circle of the governments which are united in the war. It was the U.S. Government itself and alone, practically, which did most of these things. However, we did have from time to time the cooperation of the British Government. We and the British were looking toward the placing of some of these people who found themselves in Persia. We have had the support of other governments, like Mexico, in its gracious movement to receive 5,000 of these refugees there. But by and large it was the United States and has been the U.S. Government which has formulated the policy and which carried it into execution and that has been instrumental in arranging the set-up in this country. We have taken into this country since the beginning of the Hitler regime and the persecution of the Jews, until today, approximately 580,000 refugees. . . .

You are faced now with a resolution which "urges the creation by the President of a commission of diplomatic, economic, and military experts to formulate and effectuate a plan of immediate action designed to save the surviving Jewish people of Europe from extinction at the hands of Nazi Germany."

Everybody that I know, everybody in the Department of State, and everybody that I have come in contact with is interested, and a lot of them have been active in endeavoring to save the Jewish people from the terrorism of the Nazis. . . . [Y]our committee will want to consider whether you should take a step which might be construed as a repudiation of the acts of the executive branch of your own Government, or whether any action on your part would be interpreted as a repudiation of the cause of the Jews.[10]

*   *   *

Long's testimony, combined with Wise's, persuaded the committee members to oppose the resolution. However, fearful that voting against the resolution might be perceived by the public as voting against the rescue of innocent victims of Nazism, the congressmen quietly shelved the resolution without a formal vote. At the same time, they obtained Long's permission to make public his testimony, which had been given behind closed doors. Long, confident that the transcript would put the final nail in the resolution's coffin, readily agreed. His testimony was released on December 10. The New York Times *ran a major front-page article headlined "580,000 Refugees Admitted to United States in Decade."[11] It was the most prominent coverage the* Times *ever accorded, or would accord, to Holocaust-related news. But it was based on a lie. The actual number of Jewish refugees admitted was less than one-third of Long's figure.*

Two leading political affairs journals, The Nation *and* The New Republic, *refuted Long's statistics. House Immigration Committee chair Samuel Dickstein strongly criticized Long, as did Congressman Emanuel Celler, who blasted Long's professions of sympathy for Jewish victims of Hitler as "crocodile tears," demanded that he explain "how many Jews were admitted during the last three years in comparison with the number seeking entrance," and urged him to resign. Mainstream Jewish organizations, such as the American Jewish Conference and World Jewish Congress, denounced Long. Even the conservative American Jewish Committee, which normally refrained from public protests, issued a statement citing Immigration and Naturalization Service figures that contradicted Long.*[12]

Long hoped his testimony would bury the rescue issue, but instead it ignited a fresh, and even louder, debate over the administration's harsh policy toward Jewish refugees. The growing controversy energized the resolution's supporters, including those on the Senate Foreign Relations Committee. Dorothy Detzer, the Washington, D.C., representative of the Women's International League for Peace and Freedom, later recalled the lobbying effort for the resolution and assessed its chances for passage:[13]

I found that on many questions I disagreed profoundly with Peter Bergson, though there was always logic in his point of view provided one accepted his premises. But in spite of disagreement on many matters, I was convinced that on the crucial question of rescuing Jews from the occupied countries Bergson's plans were sound. The policies of those other Jewish groups, with which I felt in more general sympathy, did not, it seemed to me, approach this problem with nearly as much clarity and directness. For Peter Bergson had sharpened the focus of his Emergency Committee to one objective. On that it concentrated; on that Peter Bergson hammered. "The problem is not how to save the Jews," he would reiterate with tireless persistence. "The problem is only where to send them when they've been rescued." . . .

I cooperated with the Emergency Committee in every way that I could. Its directions were charted by officials of the government who had the courage to join and by members of the Congress who were vitally interested. Senator Gillette, with eleven other senators, and Will Rogers in the House introduced companion resolutions in Congress which called on the Administration to create "a commission of diplomatic, economic, and military experts to formulate and effectuate a plan of immediate action designed to save the Jewish people of Europe from extinction at the hands of the Nazi government."

An active and vigorous campaign of lobbying was initiated at once: hearings, interviews, publicity, persuading, explaining—for months, the Capitol was the seat of unremitting pressure. I had other Congressional irons in the fire, but I helped the Emergency Committee as much as I could. Finally, toward the middle of January, a poll of both houses promised a sufficient margin of votes to insure passage. The measure was then slated for the calendar, and on Monday, January 24th, it was scheduled to come up for vote.

The political wind does not blow where it listeth; it runs along the ground. Now its murmur carried to the Administration the angry rumblings of the grass roots. The country, no longer indifferent to the plight of the Jews, was roused to a fever of indignation over the government's failure to act to save them. If that bill went through the Congress, Republicans might be able to take equal credit with the Democrats for forcing through this humanitarian move. For [Senator] Bob Taft's name was on the measure [as a co-sponsor], and his skill and energy behind it. Hence, its successful passage would be due in part to the minority party.[14]

* * *

Excerpts from remarks by Senator Guy Gillette at a testimonial dinner of the Emergency Committee to Save the Jewish People of Europe, New York City, 1944:[15]

[In the autumn of 1943,] I was asked to attend a meeting, along with Mrs. Gillette, in Washington, that was called by the Emergency Committee to Save the Jewish People of Europe. I told her and I told them that if this was just to be another meeting where expressions of horror were to be the order of the day, and resolutions of sympathy passed, they could just as well call the meeting of the Ladies' Aid Society . . . fortunately, my friends, I found that this group wanted to do something definite, concrete, and tangible. (Applause)

They asked me if I would introduce in the Senate a resolution for action by this nation in setting up an official body that might not only develop the factual situation but might investigate all the avenues and possibilities of assistance, realizing that these victims were under the control and in the territories that were under the control of those that were destroying them. The Congressman from California, Will Rogers, said he would introduce it in the House. I agreed to introduce it in the Senate. We prepared and offered the resolution. It was referred, in the Senate, to the Foreign Relations Committee, of which I happen to be a member.

Within twenty-four hours after the introduction of that resolution, I began to have a series of callers, not only phone calls, but personal calls; first calling my attention to the fact that those who had asked me to sponsor the resolution did not represent the Jewish people; that they were upstarts; they were just a little group who desired to aggrandize themselves and were not in a position to represent the American people of Jewish extraction.

I told them that I didn't care whom they represented. It did not make a particle of difference to me whom they represented. They said to me, "Why, Senator, we know that if you had realized who were the sponsors of this proposal, you would not have lent yourself to the introduction of the resolution."

And from that time on, these people used every effort, every means at their disposal, to block the resolution. I have told this before; I tell it to you now: that on the day that I was to call it up in the Foreign Relations Committee and we had the vote to report it out unanimously (I had already contacted every member), one of the cosponsors came in and said: "I wish these damned Jews would make up their minds what they want. I could not get inside the committee room without being buttonholed out here in the corridor by representatives who said that the Jewish people of America did not want the passage of this resolution." And he was one of the cosponsors; one of the great Senators of the United States.

That committee reported it out unanimously. Within a couple of days, or three days, I think it was, the President took the action setting up the War Refugee Board.

*   *   *

Excerpts from a meeting of the Treasury Department staff, January 13, 1944, concerning the idea of asking the President to create a "War Refugee Committee" with Morgenthau as one of its three leaders:[16]

MR. LUXFORD: Mr. Secretary, we can indicate to you projects that are on the griddle right now that, if you had a [rescue] committee of this character you might be very successful.

H.M.JR: That is the suggestion of the original committee—this is the Crowley, Stettinius, Morgenthau?

MR. LUXFORD: Right. But if you had that kind of an organization there are projects on the fire right now where you could make a real contribution, and I can list them for you right now if you want them. But that is an altogether different thing from saying what can you do in your capacity as Secretary of the Treasury, going hat in hand, to Mr. Hull. You won't get anything on these projects with those, but you can do it if you are in this committee.

MR. WHITE: You will get a specific question [from President Roosevelt], "Well, Henry, what did you want me to do, and I will do it," which is exactly the approach that will lead to very meager results, and will mean that you will have to keep constantly on the ball and get very little.

MR. PAUL: That ties in with Connally's and Bloom's objections to this Senate bill?

H.M.JR: What is that?

MR. LUXFORD: We can give you a little background on that. There have been hearings before both the House and the Senate on the ridiculous operations of State on the refugee problem. The Senate Foreign Relations Committee reported out unanimously a resolution calling for the establishment of a commission by the President to take this thing out of State and to handle the Jewish refugee problem.

Now, the House Foreign Relations Committee, Bloom's committee, had been holding hearings on the same problem, and Bloom is having to do everything he can possibly do to keep that resolution from being reported out of the House Foreign Relations Committee. Now, Bloom—

H.M.JR: Why shouldn't it be?

MR. LUXFORD: Bloom has only these two things in mind, apparently: One, that he was in on the Bermuda Conference, he was the delegate—the case reflects on that; and secondly, he probably feels that it will be a blow to the Administration to have this thing thrown out onto the Floor of the House and debated on the basis that it will be debated. It will not be any pleasant thing.

Mr. Paul: Therefore, [our] remedy is an Executive Order—let's do it without a statute.

* * *

Excerpts from an account by Nahum Goldmann, cochairman of the World Jewish Congress, of his conversation with U.S. Representative Sol Bloom, chairman of the House Foreign Affairs Committee, in December 1943:[17]

The Rogers–Gillette Resolution: Congressman Bloom said that the evidence of Dr. Wise before the Committee was excellent. He said that Mr. Breckinridge Long had made an extensive report to the Committee, which is to be published in complete form, so that the public may be informed of the efforts of the British and American governments and the Intergovernmental Committee concerning the rescue of Jews. The report indicates that every conceivable effort was made and, therefore, there is really no necessity for the Commission proposed in the Rogers Resolution. Moreover, the setting up of such a Commission would practically put all the responsibility for rescue on the American government, releasing the British and other governments from their responsibilities in this matter; in addition, it is contrary to the policy fixed at Bermuda to enlarge the Intergovernmental Committee and to channelize all the rescue work through it. He believes that the Committee will not report the resolution out, and that will be the end of it.

* * *

Meanwhile, although the Gillette–Rogers rescue resolution was shelved in the House, it was advancing in the Senate.

Kook:[18] [Bloom] pigeonhole[d] it and it never came up for a vote in the House. But it passed unanimously in the Senate Foreign Relations Committee. Even though, once the House started hearings, the Senate was supposed to wait for it. And we couldn't get the Chairman, Tom Connally (D-Texas) to take it up. And then we waited until one day he was sick—he was an old man—and the acting chairman was Senator [Elbert] Thomas (D-Utah), who was an intellectual Mormon, religious man. And as a religious man, he planned it all. He was the man who told me, "Wait, one day I'll preside and it will pass unanimously." And it did. He said, "There's no opposition to this resolution. On the contrary, we all feel that it should be done." And it passed.

* * *

With the Senate version of the resolution scheduled to be voted upon by the full Senate on January 24, and with the conflict between Long, Congress, and the Jewish community escalating, Secretary Morgenthau consulted with his staff on how to proceed.

Excerpts from a meeting of the Treasury Department staff, January 15, 1944:[19]

H.M.Jr: Oscar, for me, as well as for everybody here, give us the status of this resolution on the Hill. Where would that fit into the picture?

Mr. Cox: It would fit in this way: The Senate Foreign Relations Committee, with ten members present, voted unanimously to report the resolution out, so the only problem now is the debate on the Floor. Most of the people who know about the resolution feel that when it gets to the Floor two things will probably happen. One element thinks the resolution will be passed; the other that in the course of debate State Department's position will be ripped open in that Breckinridge Long's testimony will be attacked in the specific context that his figures were wrong, in that his facts were wrong, and it was an attempt to sugarcoat an action when action should have been taken.

On the House side the Committee has had a terrific internal fight between—le[d] in the main on one side by Will Rogers, who is one of the introducers of the resolution, and Gillette, and on the other side by Sol Bloom, who feels that a large part of this is direct personal criticism of him and what he did as the American delegate to the Bermuda Conference.

Now, Bloom, himself, although he takes a personal emotional interest in the thing, feels it would be a problem to have the full debate both on the Floors of the Senate and the House, because he doesn't think he could hold the resolution in the House Committee, and it would also be a direct attack on the Administration, including the President, for having failed to act in this kind of an important situation, so Bloom, himself, is championing to go to Hull and say, for practical reasons—and we might also call them political reasons involving the State Department, the President, and the House Foreign Affairs Committee—"I think you ought to take some bold, imaginative action such as appointing a high-level Government committee to take hold of this thing and do something about it." . . .

H.M.JR: . . . I personally hate to say this thing, but our strongest out [with the President] is the imminence of Congress doing something. That is our strongest out. Really, when you get down to the point, this is a boiling pot on the Hill. You can't hold it; it is going to pop, and you have either got to move very fast, or the Congress of the United States will do it for you. . . .

MR. COHEN:[20] . . . [T]here is not only the danger that the thing will get out of hand in Congress, but there has been the fact that, I think, Long admits, that he made a very unfortunate statement before the Congressional Committee. The story I hear is that it was prepared for him and he didn't realize that it wasn't accurate. But all that indicates that something has to be done to give the thing a fresh start, and there is also a factor which you don't want to put in the memorandum which will influence the President and influence Hull. We all know that during this political year minorities are being exploited. It is not that the minorities are trying to exploit politics. There may be some of that, but all the politicians are trying to exploit the value of minority groups, and the situation has gotten to the point where something has to be done.

* * *

PEHLE:[21] We had a meeting Sunday afternoon [January 16, 1944] at the White House in the Oval Office and the President was there, Secretary Morgenthau, Randolph Paul, and I. We gave the President the memorandum to him, but he largely listened, rather than reading the memorandum. And Secretary Morgenthau left it to me to explain why we were there, and why we felt that a separate agency outside the State Department was essential. The President asked questions and was very interested. And at the end of the meeting, the President said, "We will do it."

When the War Refugee Board was established by an Executive Order signed by President Roosevelt . . . it was drafted in the Treasury. And it was called the War Refugee Board—at no point in the Executive Order is the word Jew mentioned. But basically, that was what we were dealing with, was Jewish refugees.

Q: Who decided to do that?

PEHLE: We felt that it was easier that way to get it approved and signed.

* * *

Almost as soon as the War Refugee Board was established, a dispute erupted among the rescue advocates as to which organizations deserved credit for helping to bring about the board's creation. The Bergson Group, in its statements and publications, contended that its activities in Washington, particularly the Gillette–Rogers resolution, were the key factor. Some prominent newspapers agreed. A Christian Science Monitor *editorial characterized the establishment of the board as "the outcome of pressure brought to bear by the Emergency Committee to Save the Jewish People of Europe, a group made up of both Jews and non-Jews that has been active in the capital in recent months."*[22] *A* Washington Post *editorial concluded that in view of the Bergson Group's "industrious spadework," the group should be cited as one of the forces that was "entitled to credit for the President's forehanded move."*[23]

Mainstream Jewish leaders, however, saw it differently. Congress Weekly, *organ of Stephen Wise's American Jewish Congress, traced the creation of the board to rescue proposals that established Jewish organizations had made during the preceding year.* Congress Weekly *also took a swipe at the Bergson activists, expressing hope that the creation of the board might "serve to purge our own internal life of the plague of self-styled voluntary saviors whose chief accomplishment is the creation of confusion and bewilderment."*[24]

The perspective of the Treasury staff was articulated during several meetings of Morgenthau with his aides in the spring of 1944, in which they analyzed the factors leading to the establishment of the board.

* * *

Excerpts from a meeting of the Treasury Department staff, March 8, 1944:[25]

H.M.JR: [T]he thing that made it possible to get the President really to act on this thing—we are talking here among ourselves—was the thing that—the resolution at least had passed the Senate to form this kind of a War Refugee Committee, hadn't it? Bloom was holding it. It was reported out, wasn't it?

MR. DUBOIS: Reported out, yes.

MR. PEHLE: It was public pressure, too.

MR. DUBOIS: It was more because of what you did than anything else, in my opinion.

H.M.Jr: I had something to do with it, granted, but the tide was running with me.

Mr. DuBois: That is true.

H.M.Jr: I think that six months before I couldn't have done it. Now what I am leading up to is this: I am just wondering who the crowd is that got the thing that far.

Mr. Pehle: That is the emergency committee, Peter Bergson and his group.

* * *

Excerpt from Secretary Morgenthau's account of his recent meeting with U.S. diplomat Myron Taylor, at a meeting of the Treasury Department staff, March 16, 1944:[26]

H.M.Jr: I said, "Let's call a spade a spade. I don't think Mr. Hull has known anything about this thing, but at the lower level, our State Department and the British Foreign Office just weren't interested. Now we have a group together, and we are a little bit more frank, if you know about the Resolution in the House and in the Senate by which we forced the President to appoint a Committee [the War Refugee Board]."

I said, "A part of the thing was in order not to have the President's hand forced where he has shown so much interest in this thing and getting it started under his own free will—not to have him forced by Congress to do this."

He said, "That is right."

* * *

Excerpts from a meeting of the Treasury Department staff, May 24, 1944:[27]

H.M.Jr: What I wanted to see you people about was, I wanted a little discussion. I have been doing a little kidding around town about this Bergson. Every time I kidded about it, everybody gets so excited, so I stopped kidding. And I just wanted to know where the President's refugee group stands, versus Bergson.

Mr. Pehle: What do you mean, where we stand?

H.M.Jr: Just that. What is our contact with him and what are we doing with him and what is he doing with us.

Where do we stand officially and unofficially? I would like to know where we're at, so in case somebody like General Greenbaum,[28] or anybody else, hits me on the thing, I want to be able to know what is the position officially and unofficially, of you people here before me versus Bergson. Officially first.

Mr. Pehle: Two phases to that. One is the phase of the Emergency Committee. The Emergency Committee to Save the Jewish People of Europe was Bergson's brainchild. He has spark plugged the whole thing. Now, he had associated with him a small group of other young Palestinian Jews, but undoubtedly the impetus largely came from him. They particularly used propaganda devices of various sorts, including large full-page advertisements in newspapers, to stir up the people in the United States on the problem and to bring pressure on the Government to act. As such, as far as I can tell, they were quite successful. They got various prominent people associated with them, and they got a great deal of publicity, and they brought considerable pressure on Congress to pass a resolution which called for the setting up of an agency such as the War Refugee Board, which was ultimately set up. And their whole activity has been devoted toward bringing home to the American people generally, not just to the Jews, but generally, the facts as to what was happening.

H.M.JR: May I interrupt you? The first time that that thing was suggested to me was a memorandum from Oscar Cox last June or July. Now it goes back to last June and July that Oscar wrote me such a memorandum.

MR. PEHLE: You mean about a committee being set up?

H.M.JR: Yes.

MR. PEHLE: When they started their agitation for that, I don't know. But at least at the time the Board was finally created in January 1944, there had been pending in the Congress for many months, at least, resolutions calling for the setting up of a separate body outside the State Department, consisting of diplomatic, military and other.

MR. ABRAHAMSON:[29] If I can interrupt, I think actually they began their ads by June of last year and probably in April or May.

H.M.JR: I wonder whether Cox gave them the idea or whether they got it from him.

MR. ABRAHAMSON: I can recall it because in April or May when I was still in private agency work they published one about Romania which caused a great deal of excitement in New York.[30]

MR. PEHLE: Was that tied in with the setting up of a committee?

MR. ABRAHAMSON: No.

MR. PEHLE: At least they have been in the field now for some time.

MR. DUBOIS: They certainly made a contribution toward the establishment of the Board.

MR. PEHLE: Even the people who hate them agree they made a substantial contribution in stirring up public opinion here. I don't think there can be any legitimate question about that.

MR. LUXFORD: Those people, too, recognize that the thing that Bergson's crowd did that was most significant was to say that this problem is one for the American people and not the Jews. In other words, the Jewish groups have been appealing to Jewish individuals, organizations, whereas this group said, "This is the responsibility of the American people, all of them, to see that action is taken." And even the other groups have acknowledged that that was an important step that they took.

*   *   *

Q:[31] What was your impression of Peter Bergson?

DUBOIS: Peter and I got along very well. As a matter of fact, I also knew his wife before they were married, and after they married. When she died, he asked me to make a little talk, along with the rabbi, at the funeral. I'm very fond of Peter and I think he probably feels pretty good towards me. But there are two views on

Peter, as you probably have gotten. I think he did a lot of good, historically. There were times I think he went too far, but that's not necessarily bad. But I think he did a lot of good in the overall program. I think a lot of his activities, in terms of advertisements, put a lot of pressure on the government, particularly before the formation of the War Refugee Board. It all helped create an atmosphere. So I think Peter's activities were helpful. I know the Jewish organizations hated his guts. But that to me was a terrible situation. Trying to save people, and they were opposing the program just because Peter recommended it. It got so ridiculous.

Notes

1. Henry Morgenthau III interview with Josiah E. DuBois, Jr., Pitman, NJ, 26 February 1981, transcript in the possession of the author.

2. Joan Morgenthau, M.D., the daughter of Henry Morgenthau, Jr., was interviewed by Martin Ostrow in Cambridge, MA, on 13 January 1992. This is an excerpt from that interview.

3. Martin Ostrow interview with John Pehle, Bethesda, Maryland, 2 October 1991.

4. Laurence Jarvik interview with Josiah E. DuBois, Jr., Camden, NJ, on 23 October 1978.

5. Morgenthau Diaries [hereafter MD], Franklin D. Roosevelt Presidential Library, Hyde Park, NY, 693/188–211.

6. Herbert E. Gaston, a former editor at the *New York World* and founder of the Federated Press service, was chief of public relations for the Treasury Department under Morgenthau.

7. *Problems of World War II and Its Aftermath*, Part 2, Selected Executive Session Hearings of the Committee, 1943–50 (Washington, D.C.: U.S. House of Representatives, 1976), 15–16. Bergson Group activist Fowler Harper, a law professor and solicitor for the Department of the Interior, drafted the legislation. See Harper to Gillette, 1 November 1943, and Rogers to Shetzer, 6 November 1943, File 1/7/1–11 Het, Folder: Emergency Committee to Save the Jewish People of Europe—Resolutions, Bergson Group collection, Jabotinsky Institute, Tel Aviv.

8. Frances Gunther (1897–1964), author and journalist, was active with the Bergson Group from its earliest days, when it was known as the American Friends of a Jewish Palestine. She was married until 1944 to John Gunther, author of *Death Be Not Proud* and other books.

9. *Problems of World War II and Its Aftermath*, Part 2, 220.

10. *Problems of World War II and Its Aftermath*, Part 2, 171, 181–182.

11. Frederick R. Barkley, "580,000 Refugees Admitted to United States in Decade," *New York Times*, 11 December 1943, 1.

12. David S. Wyman, *The Abandonment of the Jews: America and the Holocaust, 1941–1945* (New York: Pantheon, 1984), 195–198; Laurel Leff, *Buried by the Times: The Holocaust and America's Most Important Newspaper* (New York: Cambridge University Press, 2005), 259–260.

13. Dorothy Detzer, *Appointment on the Hill* (New York: Henry Holt & Co., 1948), 241–242.

14. The co-sponsors in the Senate, in addition to Gillette, were Republicans Robert Taft (Ohio) and Homer Ferguson (Michigan), and Democrats Elbert Thomas (Utah), Edwin Johnson (Colorado), Bennett Champ Clark (Missouri), Sheridan Downey (California), Allen Ellender (Louisiana), Joseph Guffey (Pennsylvania), James Murray (Montana), George Radcliffe (Maryland), and Frederick Van Nuys (Indiana).

15. Bergson Group collection, The David S. Wyman Institute for Holocaust Studies, Washington, D.C.

16. MD 693/188–211.

17. The meeting took place on December 8, 1943; Goldmann's account may be found in Folder I-80, Abba Hillel Silver Papers, the Temple, Cleveland, OH.

18. Laurence Jarvik interview with Hillel Kook, New York, NY, 10 November 1978.

19. MD 694/88–90, 94–97.

20. Presidential adviser Ben Cohen was evidently referring to the possibility that the Republicans would exploit the refugee crisis as a means of luring Jewish voters in the November 1944 presidential contest. Jews comprised an estimated 14 percent of the population of New York State which, with its forty-seven electoral votes, played a decisive role in presidential campaign politics. (With one exception, no candidate had been elected president since 1876 without carrying New York.) Although Jewish voters were generally assumed to be in Roosevelt's pocket—80 to 90 percent of Jewish voters had backed FDR in his three previous presidential races—the leading contenders for the Republican presidential nomination, Wendell Willkie and Thomas Dewey, were actively pursuing Jewish votes. Willkie publicly endorsed the goal of Jewish statehood, and Dewey appeared at a Zionist rally in New York in November 1943 and called for the opening of Palestine to all Jewish refugees. In his diary, Vice President Henry Wallace worried about "how vigorously Willkie is going to town for Palestine."

   In a similar vein, when Winston Churchill met with Roosevelt earlier that year and FDR spoke of the need to maintain good relations with the Arab countries, Churchill replied that "there were more Jewish than Arab votes in the Anglo-Saxon countries and we could not afford to ignore such practical considerations." John L. Blum, *The Price of Vision: The Diaries of Henry A. Wallace, 1942–1946* (Boston: Houghton Mifflin, 1973), 313.

21. Ostrow interview with Pehle, op. cit.

22. *Christian Science Monitor*, 24 January 1944.

23. *Washington Post*, 25 January 1944.

24. "The Task of Rescue," *Congress Weekly*, 11 February 1944, 3.

25. MD 707/220–221.

26. MD 710/194.

27. MD 735/224–26.

28. Edward S. Greenbaum (1890–1970), a New York attorney, U.S. Naval officer, and prominent member of the American Jewish Committee, was an old friend of Morgenthau's, with whom he sometimes discussed Jewish affairs.

29. Treasury Department staff member James Abrahamson.

30. Evidently a reference to "FOR SALE to Humanity: 70,000 Jews, Guaranteed Human Beings at $50 a Piece," op. cit. For background on the controversy over this ad, see

David S. Wyman and Rafael Medoff, *A Race against Death: Peter Bergson, America, and the Holocaust* (New York: The New Press, 2002), 30–31.

The first Bergson Group newspaper ad mentioning the idea of creating a rescue agency was published in the *Washington Post* on April 20, 1943 (10), headlined "To the Gentlemen at Bermuda . . ." It called for "the immediate creation of a United Nations Agency, of military and diplomatic experts, with full authority to determine and effectuate a realistic and stern policy of action, to save the remaining millions of Jewish people who are marked for cold-blooded slaughter by Hitler." The shift from seeking a "United Nations Agency" to a specifically American government agency was first articulated in the resolutions of the Bergson Group's July 1943 Emergency Conference to Save the Jewish People of Europe. The first resolution stated: "The Government of the United States is urged to create an official agency specifically charged with the task of saving the Jewish people of Europe. The other United Nations should be invited to participate in this agency, with a view to its ultimate conversion into a United Nations agency; but, because of the urgency of the problem, action should not be postponed pending the adherence of other nations." Resolution reprinted in Yitshaq Ben-Ami, *Years of Wrath, Days of Glory* (New York: Shengold, 1983), 574–575.

31. Richard Breitman and Alan Kraut interview with Josiah E. DuBois, Jr., Camden, NJ, 12 October 1982.

CHAPTER FIVE

The War Refugee Board in Action

On January 22, 1944, two days before the Gillette–Rogers rescue resolution was scheduled for a vote before the full Senate, President Roosevelt issued Executive Order 9417 establishing the War Refugee Board.[1] Gillette and Rogers promptly withdrew their resolution. Since Morgenthau and his aides had played such a key role in bringing the board into existence, it is not surprising that the board became essentially a Treasury operation, even if technically it was an intradepartmental agency. The board's office was located in the Treasury Department building, and Pehle, DuBois, and their colleagues became its senior staff. It was a transformative moment in the history of America's response to the Holocaust. For the first time, there was a U.S. government agency whose sole purpose was to rescue Jews from Hitler.

* * *

PEHLE:[2] The issuance of the Executive Order establishing the War Refugee Board was the turning point in that it changed the policy of the United States to one of affirmatively helping refugees instead of suppressing the information as to what was going on. . . . But we were established late, we had limited resources, and we had to work with other departments that weren't necessarily as anxious as we were to move forward.

There were many things that could be done. We could provide service to the private [refugee] agencies [in Europe] and we could let them send money into Switzerland in ways that didn't give any foreign exchange to the Germans. We could see that the Germans were warned repeatedly that the crimes against the Jews wouldn't be forgotten after the war. And this became more important and more effective as the war drew to a close when even the Germans could see they were going to lose. Early in the game, they thought they could conquer the world. They wouldn't

John Pehle, first director of the War Refugee Board, in the 1940s.

pay too much attention to warnings. But at this point, the warnings tended to strike home.[3]

* * *

Q:[4] What was your role in the War Refugee Board?

DuBois: I became the general counsel of the War Refugee Board, and John Pehle became the director of the War Refugee Board. Now, the War Refugee Board was composed of the Secretary of State, the Secretary of the Treasury and the Secretary of War, but it was . . . run by the Treasury Department. John Pehle ran this whole show, recruited his own men, many from the—in fact, most from the Treasury Department.

* * *

I. The Fainting Rabbi

DuBois:[5] One of the first things that came to my attention as general counsel on the War Refugee Board was Secretary Morgenthau received a request from a group of Jewish rabbis, for an interview late one afternoon [Thursday, April 6, 1944]. He asked me to be present.

These Jewish rabbis, who incidentally were headed by . . . Rabbi [Baruch] Korff,[6] came to Secretary Morgenthau's office and many of them literally cried. And they described the fact that there were 238 Jewish rabbis who had arrived at an internment camp in France with passports to Latin American countries, and in order to get to these Latin American countries, it was necessary to pass through the United States.

The State Department had taken the position that these Latin American passports were forged and they were not going to let these people through the United States. Secretary Morgenthau was so shocked that he attempted immediately to get Secretary Hull on the phone, but he had left. He tried to get Sumner Welles, but he had left for the day. And so there we were at that point practically helpless.

* * *

Rabbi Baruch Korff:[7] Representative John W. McCormack,[8] Majority Leader of the U.S. House of Representatives, arranged for [us] to see Henry Morgenthau . . . on April 6, 1944. . . .

[Also at the meeting was] John W. Pehle, Executive Director of the [War Refugee] Board, who surprisingly enough used the opportunity to denounce "State Department obstructionists" who in his own words, "paralyze the Board."

Morgenthau wanted to know "why McCormack, a Catholic, is on such friendly terms with a rabbi?" "I have to make a plane in a half-hour," he said, "but John insisted, first in a telegram, then over the telephone, that I see you at once. I don't want to sound impatient. As a matter of fact, these things should have been brought to my attention long ago and I am intrigued by your relationship with John, but please, be brief!"

The Secretary was very attentive. He canceled his flight and spent more than three hours with us, during which the differences with the State Department were aired out. Josiah DuBois, Counsel General of the Board, who joined us at Pehle's request, informed the Secretary of the latest development. He detailed an incident that portrayed the opposition we had to face.

On April 4, two of Mr. Pehle's assistants, Lawrence Lesser and James Mann, met with three State Department officials, whom DuBois identified as Paul T. Culbertson, Head of the Western European Division; James H. Keely, Chief of the Special War Division; and George Warren, Advisor on Refugees and Displaced Persons. Mr. Keely was bizarre in his fury against the refugees with Latin-American passports; he abruptly announced to Lesser and Mann that "Joseph P. Kennedy, former U.S. Ambassador to London, advised the State Department that the Jews at Camp Vittel and those interned elsewhere secured their passports from the Gestapo. There is reason to assume that they are enemy agents." Keely let it be known that he and higher echelons had tabled the Board's cable of February 21 and the subsequent cable of March 16, which directed Harrison, the U.S. Minister to Bern, to intercede.

* * *

KLOTZ:[9] There was this rabbi [who] asked for an appointment. Now, I was not the appointments secretary. . . . [H]e gave this man, Rabbi Kalmanowitz,[10] that was

Rabbi Avraham Kalmanowitz (at left) during a march by 400 rabbis to the White House in October 1943, to urge President Roosevelt to rescue Jewish refugees.

his name, an appointment and Rabbi Kalmanowitz didn't speak a word of English, so he said, and he brought with him a rabbi [Korff] who did speak English and he was going to translate, you know. [Korff, Kalmanowitz, and a third rabbi, Aharon Kotler] came and they wanted—it was a time when all foreign funds were frozen and [they] came to [Morgenthau]. They wanted to bring out some very, very important rabbis from Poland and he wanted some money unfrozen because he—they had to bribe them. They couldn't get anything done unless you bribed them. And [they] told them the truth.

* * *

KALMANOWITZ:[11] [I am c]oming to you Mr. Secretary about saving the lives of the Jewish [sic]. We have a question from 2,238 interned people in the camps of Vittel and Tittmoning.

We received yesterday by cable that every inmate there is in danger of life and death.

We come to the office of Mr. Pehle, and Mr. Pehle, I know very well, in the four or six weeks or less that he is working very hard to save the lives . . . Mr. Lesser, Miss Hodel and Mr. DuBois, who are willing to work day and night for the saving—I know very well and I recognize—the saving has not come. I don't know about the blame. I think the blame is in the State Department. There is every danger not only for the lives of the 2,238 people, but for three and a half million people. We have not very much help.

Please Mr. Secretary do the utmost that you can do to save them, every one. . . .

I know Mr. Lesser and Hodel[12] and DuBois have at hand three cables that must go yesterday, and the cables are not going; one cable to Spain, one cable to the Swiss, one cable to the South American countries. You know very well, the less cables you have to send through the State Department[, the better].

* * *

KLOTZ:[13] Well, most rabbis were this big [raises her hand slightly to indicate the height of a short person] but this Kalmanowitz was six foot tall, the most handsome man you ever saw. And they did not know that I was Jewish and that I spoke the language and I understood. Well, we spoke both. We spoke German and we spoke Yiddish. My mother really learned Yiddish after she came to America but were taught both, German and Yiddish. So that when Kalmanowitz arrived the translator told [Morgenthau] what I just told you, they wanted money and funds unfrozen and so on. And Kalmanowitz answered him, he said "press him more, he looks like the kind you can get away with an awful lot of things," words to that effect. And then [Morgenthau] said, "Well, gentlemen, I will have to take it under advisement and speak to my subordinate, you see." And Kalmanowitz said to his interpreter, "Once you hear the word 'taking it under advisement,' forget it. He's going to do nothing," or words to that effect.

And I heard all this and with that, just at that point, Kalmanowitz falls on the floor and goes into a faint. And [Morgenthau] was very sensitive. He had a lot of buttons to push when he wanted this one and this one, Secret Service. He pushed all the buttons and the Secret Service came in with a gun and all this happened. And then I thought he fainted, too, I mean, I had a suspicion and the next thing that happened—a nurse and a doctor revived him and [Morgenthau] said, "Henrietta, take him out the private entrance, get him into my car and get him back to his hotel."

And so I went out into the little private entrance, and Rabbi Kalmanowitz said [in Yiddish], "Did I cry well?" He said this to the other rabbi. And the other rabbi said, "*Sehr gut, sehr gut* [Very well, very well]." And I almost died when I heard this and of course I wouldn't tell [Morgenthau] because if I told it to him, he would never let another rabbi in. And I am Jewish, and his cause was justified. It wasn't that he was a crook and wanted the money to get away with it.

Q: Did you let the rabbi know that you knew what he was saying?

KLOTZ: No, I didn't say a word. I didn't look Jewish at that time. I was young and I was very, very blond and they didn't know I was Jewish, and I didn't say a word.

Many years later, [Morgenthau] and [Henry] Montor [of Israel Bonds], it was early, about 8:30 in the morning and they were talking, planning things and I was home sick for a couple of days and I came in and looked at the calendar and I see Rabbi Kalmanowitz. And I said, "What does he want?" and [Morgenthau] said to me, "Every time you hear that man's name, you curdle." So I thought to myself, it's about time now that I tell him what happened. . . . And when I told him the story, Montor laughed so hard, he fell off his chair. I'm not exaggerating. He just thought that was the funniest thing and [Morgenthau] said, "Henrietta, you should have told me the truth." I said, "I'm entitled to one lie in my life and this was it. I couldn't tell you. You would have misunderstood. This man was trying to do anything to get these—what he thought were important rabbis, and they were."

*   *   *

RABBI LEVI HOROWITZ:[14] Rabbi Kalmanowitz was our next door neighbor on Bedford Avenue in Brooklyn. There was that famous Shabbos when he got people to collect money for the Jews in Europe. Of course, people who knew him understood that if he was asking for money [on the Sabbath, when Jewish religious law prohibits handling money except in a life-and-death situation], it was because he wanted people to recognize the seriousness of the situation. . . . It seemed strange to be collecting money on Shabbos, but people gave him the benefit of the doubt. Sometimes, when he was speaking and making an appeal for money for the Jews in Europe, he fainted. Somebody once accused him—said his fainting was "made to order." One time, years later, he said, "Maybe it's true that when I got up to speak about the situation in Europe I was exaggerating what I knew at that moment, in order to make an impression on people—but later we found out that what really happened was far worse than any of my so-called exaggerations."

* * *

Shaken by this dramatic episode with Rabbi Kalmanowitz, Morgenthau telephoned the State Department, hoping to reach Secretary Hull:

KORFF:[15] After having been told that the Secretary of State, Cordell Hull, was conferring with the President on the Big Four Foreign Ministers' meeting which he had attended in Moscow, Morgenthau telephoned the Undersecretary of War, Robert Paterson. Paterson promised to call back after checking with Assistant Secretary of War John J. McCloy, who was assigned by Secretary Stimson to deal with all matters pertaining to the War Refugee Board.

Throughout the late afternoon, Morgenthau attempted to reach Hull by telephone. He was told that Secretary Hull was tied up preparing an address scheduled for radio delivery Sunday evening April 9. . . . [B]efore the day was over, Hull dispatched George Warren to Morgenthau's office. The Secretary was impatient with Warren; he seemed to feel that the Secretary of State had sent an "errand boy" to pacify him.

* * *

At a Treasury Department staff meeting the next day—Friday, April 7—Morgenthau recounted what happened when he reached Secretary Hull:[16]

H.M.JR: There are a little over 2,300 people in the camp at Vittel, France. They are under South American passports, which may be fraudulent or not; it doesn't make much difference. But for a month and a half the War Refugee Board has had a cable lying over there in the State Department urging them to ask the Swiss to ask the Germans to recognize these people. Well, two hundred and fifty of them have been moved, and that means death. They put them in a gas chamber, and that is that. For a month and a half it has been lying over there. And these people have been fussing around with different people in the State Department. I sat here, and finally Mr. Hull came to the phone at six o'clock. I read the thing over the phone, what we wanted. He said it sounded all right. . . .

Then he sent [George] Warren over here, who is supposed to look after it. He said, "I have no instructions; I was simply told to come here. I can't do anything; I have no instructions."

I said, "You had better get instructions."

I got word to Mr. Hull's secretary. Well, he didn't think he had better bother Mr. Hull.

I said, "You better bother him tonight. After all, if you get a cable out tonight it will be Friday morning [when it arrives]. If you don't see him until tomorrow, it will be Saturday. You get him tonight!"

Now, there are two stories, one that the cable went, and one that they are meeting at nine o'clock this morning to decide it, because they had a Policy Board meeting in the State Department yesterday in which they won't give us the language, just weasel-word stuff.

But these people [the delegation of rabbis] were sent to me with telephone calls from Senator Mead[17] and Congressman McCormack. They say if they don't get action they will call a press conference and announce it. Personally, although it isn't my suggestion, it is about time. . . .

[The reason for the State Department's delays in this matter is that t]hey don't want to do anything to help these refugees. There is a man by the name of Culbertson who has been handling it. Here is Culbertson. Just get this, see. He is the Acting Chief of European Division, and when the State Department decided without the President's knowledge that . . . there were certain things in Tunisia that we wanted done, I don't know whether it was property returned or refugees, or something. And when they decided to do it, mind you, the President didn't know anything about it; Culbertson storms out of a meeting and in the presence of a responsible person says, "Well, that damned Jew in the Treasury must have gotten to the President." That man is the Acting Chief of the European Division today.

* * *

DuBois: I was at one point told [by Donald Hiss] that another person in the State Department said that "this Jew Morgenthau and his Jewish assistant DuBois are trying to run the State Department." It so happens that I'm not Jewish.[18]

* * *

Korff:[19] On the morning of [Friday,] April 7, the cable in dispute was transmitted to Harrison without the change of a comma. Morgenthau was jubilant. I was at the office of Senator James M. Mead when he called to tell me: "We got some action after all. If there is anything else you want me to do, don't hesitate to call on me!" I did call on him, five times during the ensuing two weeks, and thereafter intermittently.

I used the authority of Jim Mead's office to pursue the Latin Ambassadors in a manner not uncommon in "diplomacy." I obtained a list of the South and Central American republics who stood to gain from legislation in one way or another, or needed Treasury clearance on a loan or some other project that could be hindered by public criticism, and I went to work as sedulously as an auditor and as unscrupulously as an extortionist.

On the morning of [Saturday,] April 8, Mr. Brown, Administrative Assistant to Secretary Hull, wired Eugene T. Kinnaly, Secretary to Representative McCormack, that arrangements had been made for me to see Mr. Hull, on Monday, April 10, at twelve fifteen o'clock. On the afternoon of the same day, Brown telephoned to cancel the meeting.

[After the information about the refugees was broadcast by the syndicated columnist and radio commentator Drew Pearson on his Sunday night radio show], Brown called Kinnaly [the next morning] to be sure "that Korff kept his appointment with the Secretary at twelve fifteen p.m."

* * *

DuBois:[20] I, for the first time, decided to take a rather drastic step. I put a call in to Drew Pearson [who] at that time had a key spot on Sunday night radio, a half hour program, in which he used to reveal many things that were leaked to him were going on in the government, and usually they were things that were obviously—needed correction. And I told Pearson briefly about the facts and he himself was so shocked he asked if he could come out to my home in Silver Spring [Maryland], which he did.

He had lunch Saturday afternoon [April 8, 1944] with my wife and I, and I gave him the details of this, and on his Sunday night broadcast, he revealed the details that I have just mentioned.

* * *

GOODWIN:[21] Someone in Joe's position certainly should not be giving information to the press without clearing it with Morgenthau. But sometimes his sense of indignation would reach a boiling point and his conscience just couldn't take it any more. At the same time, though, he had a good sense of when he could come down hard on someone and when he shouldn't push it too far, and that's one of the things that made him so effective.

* * *

Excerpt from Drew Pearson's April 9, 1944 radio broBoisadcast:[22]

On February 26, the War Refugee Board created by the President asked the State Department to send cables abroad to aid certain Jewish Refugees in French Concentration camps. The Refugees had passport visas to go to Latin America, but the Nazis were about to deport them to Poland for slaughter. So the State Department was asked to cable its representative abroad to help. That was February 26—six weeks ago. Meanwhile, President Roosevelt proclaimed that this country would aid refugees but, unfortunately, for six long weeks that cable to Europe to aid 238 people about to be shipped to Poland was held up on a State Department desk.

Finally, certain Congressmen demanded that the State Department carry out the policies of the President. So last Friday, the State Department at long last sent the cable—six weeks late.

Unfortunately, the 238 Refugees who awaited that cable may now be dead. The Congressmen who did their best to help them were Senator James Mead of New York and Representative John McCormack of Massachusetts. The men in the State Department who held up the cable were Paul Culbertson of the European Department, and James Dunn, close Advisor to Secretary Hull.

* * *

Excerpt from a meeting of State Department officials, April 10, 1944:[23]

Mr. [Green H.] Hackworth [legal adviser to the State Department] explained that he had been called to the Secretary [of State]'s office in the morning and found the Secretary concluding with certain Rabbis a conversation at which Mr. [Hayden] Rayn[o]r had been present. The Rabbis referred to certain telegrams sent over from the War Refugee Board on Saturday and stated that it was essential that those telegrams be sent out the same day. They alleged that an earlier telegram which they had sponsored had been delayed over a month in the Department and stated that they had taken the liberty of informing Mr.

Drew Pearson of the facts regarding that telegram as they understood them. It was stated that the War Refugee Board and the Rabbis had been on the telephone continuously since that time in order to determine whether the telegrams had yet gone out, that the Secretary was "on a spot," and that it was believed that the telegrams should go out unless there was something illegal about them.

* * *

At the meeting with Secretary Hull on Monday, April 10, "Hull was frigid," according to Korff. The secretary of state began the conversation by denouncing Drew Pearson's broadcast as "lies" and calling Pearson a "scandalist" and a "chronic liar."[24] *Korff's account of the rest of the conversation:*

HULL: Do you know that I am the nominal head of the War Refugee Board and no one is going to tell me how to run it.

KORFF: I had hoped that you would be that in fact and not just nominally; and that you would take an active—

HULL: You are not familiar with the many burdens of the Secretary of State. I must delegate authority to others and no one is going to tell me how to run my office. No one is going to intimidate me.

("His face tightened and his eyes dropped as his usual calm deserted him," Korff recalled. "Kotler, who didn't understand English but was restive over the Secretary's obvious anger, and Kinnaly, who meant well but didn't know what he was getting into when he volunteered to come along, shifted uneasily in their seats.")

KORFF: If I may, Mr. Secretary, I shall give you a dozen instances where your subordinates have, without cause, overridden the President's directives and made a mockery of your own good intentions.

KINNALY: Rabbi Korff is upset and troubled, he means no offense—

KORFF: With all due respect, I do not feel as if I am in need of apologists. No nation, however imbued with a sense of righteousness, can honestly afford to flaunt obligations to which it has committed itself, without forfeiting its honor. . . .

HULL (summoning his secretary): Have [Hackworth] come into my office. (turning to us) We will soon find out what this is all about.

KORFF: That's what I have been trying to tell you, Mr. Secretary.

HULL: Tell me when Mr. [Hackworth] comes in. (Mr. [Hackworth] entered while Secretary Hull twirled angrily in his chair.)

HULL: Mr. [Hackworth], do you know anything about this—this refugee business?

KORFF: I didn't come here to fence with you, Mr. Secretary. If you'll just give me the chance, I'll explain.

[HACKWORTH]: Go ahead.

Korff's account: "With all the skill and tact at my command, I appealed to him in the simplest terms, avoiding all indictment of the bigoted and benighted. Hull is not a generous man, but what he lacks in generosity he makes up in honesty. He paused at the conclusion of my plea and said: 'Well, you got your cable off, what else is there to be done?'"

KORFF: I am glad you asked me that, Mr. Secretary. There is a lot to be done. The War Refugee Board wants all the Latin American Republics who have invalidated their passports to reinstate them. Our Ambassador in Spain, Dr. Carlton J.H. Hayes, should recognize this humane endeavor, which he has not, since most of the South American countries are represented [in Germany] by Spain. Mr. [Breckinridge] Long, Mr. [Adolf] Berle and Mr.[James] Dunn and their associates should be apprised of your interest.

HULL: I recall having approved this passport ruse as an expediency measure to save human lives.

KORFF: Then it should be followed through. Any departure from this policy is likely to erase well over one hundred thousand lives. It might prove embarrassing, Mr. Secretary, were I to suggest that the United States, too, issue such protective passports.

For the first time a smile flickered over his face; he turned to Mr. [Hackworth]. "Will you personally see to it that this whole refugee matter gets attended to? Oh, yes, and tell Mr. Pehle that I want to see him!"

[HACKWORTH]: Yes, Mr. Secretary.

KOTLER (in Yiddish): Will you ask the Secretary about the Hungarian Jews?

KORFF: Now is not the time. I'll follow that up through other channels.

KORFF: Mr. Secretary, may I call you as the situation develops and your personal att—

HULL: Call Mr. [Hackworth] or Mr. Brown and be careful what you say to that gossiper. The War Refugee Board is one of many agencies and we must look to the overall objective. We can't abandon one at the expense of another.

* * *

DUBOIS:[25] Early Monday morning [April 10, 1944], Secretary Morgenthau received a call from Secretary Hull stating that the State Department was prepared to recognize these passports, but it was too late. He later learned that the 238 rabbis had been shipped back, undoubtedly to be eventually exterminated. . . .

[Morgenthau] then called me in—this was before we knew [that the 238 rabbis] had been sent back—and [he] had a wonderful way about him. He said, "Secretary Hull just called me; he said they're going to recognize those passports." And I said, "Oh, I'm glad to hear that." He said, "I guess that broadcast last night had something to do with it." I said, "It probably did." He said, "I wonder who leaked that story." I said, "Well, someone who cared must have leaked it." [Morgenthau] said no more. He didn't ask me whether I'd leaked it, or anything else. But he had a pretty good idea, I think.[26]

* * *

Excerpts from a memo by American Jewish Committee official Simon Segal, to his AJC colleague Dr. John Slawson, April 20, 1944, regarding the Vittel camp:[27]

The Jews of Poland and of other occupied countries who have succeeded in obtaining foreign passports, particularly South American passports, have been put by the Germans into several special camps for foreigners. One of the largest of these camps, containing 2,000 to 3,000 Jews, was established in Vittel, Alsace. The conditions in the Vittel camp were relatively good. Of course the Germans knew very well that the people who held the foreign passports were not citizens of those countries, but they were keeping them as hostages for the exchange of Germans held by the United Nations.

Several weeks ago I had suggested, and our Polish Advisory Committee had discussed, that the American Jewish Committee should approach the War Refugee Board and particularly the State Department. We asked that the State Department should notify, through Switzerland, the German government that at least some token exchange would be considered in the near future. Such a declaration would have saved not only the Jews who are already in the camps but would have permitted also for the sending of further passports to other Jews and the Germans would have had interest to continue to recognize the validity of these passports. Unfortunately nothing was done in the matter.

In the meantime the Agudath Israel, the Orthodox organization, had received from their people in Switzerland a telegram that there is immediate danger that the camps for foreigners, especially the camp in Vittel, will be liquidated. They went to see the people of the War Refugee Board in Washington and also talked to Breckinridge Long and others of the State Department. The State Department was noncommittal and the War Refugee Board expressly asked that the Jewish organizations should exert strong pressure upon the State Department to make a declaration that an exchange would be considered. Dr. [Isaac] Lewin of the Aguda immediately contacted us and asked us to intervene within the State Department. Mr. [Jacob] Landau[28] happened to be in Washington that day and we asked him to verify with the War Refugee Board Dr. Lewin's information. The information proved entirely correct and the War Refugee Board re-emphasized the need for pressure upon the State Department. While we were hesitating the War Refugee Board informed us that they had succeeded themselves in convincing the State Department that such a declaration was necessary for the saving of the Jews in the camps and that the State Department had instructed the American minister in Switzerland to notify the Germans through the Swiss government that the people in the camp would be considered in the future exchanges.

A few days later the Aguda received further telegrams that the camp in Vittel had already been liquidated. Two Orthodox rabbis, in spite of Passover, immediately went to Washington and through the intervention of Senator [Robert] Wagner [D-New York] and some Congressmen got to see the Secretary of State Cordell Hull. They asked him to intervene with the Spanish government, whose ambassador seems to be very influential in Berlin, to stop the liquidation of the camps. They also asked that the Jews who had already been deported from Vittel should be returned or sent to another camp for foreigners. They have succeeded in convincing Mr. Hull that this was an extremely urgent and important matter and the State Department instructed the American ambassador in Spain to intervene with the Spanish government. We await further developments and as yet no answer has been received from the Germans.

I believe we should follow very closely all further developments and do everything in our power to save the Jews in the camps for foreigners. I very much regret to say that in spite of the fact that the people of the Aguda came to us first, we have helped them very little in that extremely important matter.

* * *

PEHLE:[29] One of the most successful things [was when] we discovered that the Germans in their methodical way of operating had set up their camp in Vittel, France, for Jews who had passports from Latin American countries which they didn't think were valid. And these passports had been bought in Switzerland and other places from the representatives. These people had never been to the Latin American countries, couldn't speak the language. And the Germans then were starting to inquire about these passports or the country that ostensibly issued them.

And we got the State Department, over real troublesome objections, to cable each of our ambassadors in these countries, and say, "you should go to the [representatives of that] country and make strong representations. These passports should not be declared invalid while the war is going on." And they did that. They said these are passports.

You'd go to the legation in Berne of one of the Latin American countries and buy these passports. And these things were really not valid. But these people had a piece of paper that looked like they were citizens of that country. And therefore, they at least had some way to move and they'd gotten into France, you see. And the thing was to keep them alive and keep them in a special category because they had this passport.

And I think, you know, you saved a lot of their lives this way, despite delaying. This was late in the war. The time was coming when the Germans could see the handwriting on the wall.

* * *

II. The War Refugee Board's Operations in Spain

Q:[30] What kind of impediments did the Board face?

PEHLE: We had areas such as Spain where there was a flow of refugees over the Pyrenees from France and the Spanish government was fairly tolerant of this, but our Ambassador there, Carlton Hayes, was negative. And we had a representative in Spain but he was never able to get any real cooperation out of the Embassy. This was also true of the Vatican which wasn't helpful in the whole refugee business.[31]

* * *

Excerpts from a memo by Pehle to Morgenthau, March 27, 1944:[32]

The War Refugee Board's experience indicates clearly the absolute impossibility in the present circumstances of obtaining the cooperation of Ambassador Hayes in Spain. It demonstrates the necessity of the President's appointing and sending to Spain at once an outstanding person, preferably a Catholic, as his personal representative to handle War Refugee Board matters. This seems to be our only hope of getting anything accomplished in this most important area. It is essential that the President confer on his representative such authority that his efforts cannot be hampered by the obstinacy of Ambassador Hayes.

The following is a brief record of Hayes' refusal to cooperate with the Board:

1. At the time the Board was established, Hayes was requested by the Board and the State Department to bring the President's policy to the attention of the Spanish Government and ask whether it was prepared to cooperate. Hayes curtly refused this request, stating that it was neither necessary nor desirable to explain our policy to the Spanish Government.

2. Subsequently, both the Board and the State Department presented to Hayes a detailed plan for increasing the flow of refugees from France to Spain. Hayes was requested to present this plan to the Spanish Government with a view to securing its approval. Hayes bluntly refused. In effect he indicated that for various reasons he believes that nothing worthwhile can be done in Spain to increase the flow of refugees.

3. The Board requested Hayes' consent to designate as its representative in Spain David Blickenstaff, whom Hayes had already put in charge of all relief organizations there. Hayes replied that he did not wish Blickenstaff to spend full time on the Board's work, indicating in effect that he would not approve the appointment if Blickenstaff were required to give up his other work.

4. The Board then, in view of the absolute necessity of having a full time representative in Spain, asked Hayes' approval for the nomination of James J. Saxon, Treasury representative in North Africa, as its temporary representative. Hayes flatly rejected this suggestion, indicating that he could not understand why the Board really needed any representative in Spain. He then expressed a preference for the designation of Blickenstaff, apparently on a part time basis, if the Board insists that someone be appointed. He also took occasion to indicate his view that there is nothing the Board can do in Spain.

5. In accordance with the settled policy of the Board, a Treasury license was granted authorizing the [American Jewish Joint Distribution Committee] representative in Spain to spend up to $100,000 to evacuate refugees, principally children, from France to Spain. The license permits communication with persons in enemy territory. The Board requested Hayes to transmit a copy of this license to the JDC representative in Spain. Hayes' most recent response is a flat refusal to do so, replete with a number of irrelevant and spurious reasons which indicate that he is simply opposed to extensive refugee operations in Spain. . . .

From the record to date it is clear that Hayes does not intend to permit, if he can help it, the evacuation of any more refugees than possible from France to Spain, and that he is determined completely to bury the refugee issue, liquidating as soon as possible the very small refugee business now going on in Spain. He has rejected every request of the War Refugee Board even though such requests have had the full backing of the State Department itself. He has given as his excuse a variety of arguments which, while they may possibly sound reasonable to someone completely ignorant of the refugee problem, in reality add up to the simple fact that he intends to oppose the War Refugee Board's efforts actually to bring more people out of occupied areas into Spain.

As you know, the War Refugee Board's experience with Hayes is not the first one of its kind. You will recall that Myron Taylor voluntarily informed you that the Intergovernmental Committee had found it impossible to get any co-operation from Hayes on refugee matters. We have also been reliably informed that Hayes has made life miserable for other government agencies attempting to work in Spain. Apparently he has been responsible for having OSS representatives recalled from that country. In the refugee field he has hamstrung private organizations by making them all subject to the control of his assistant, Mr. Blickenstaff, who helped dispense relief on the Franco side during the civil war.

In the circumstances, the operations of the Board in Spain are completely paralyzed and we are losing practically the only opportunity we have at the moment for actually bringing people out of occupied territory.

*   *   *

III. The War Refugee Board's Operations in Turkey

KOOK:[33] We were submitting ads to the [New York] Times and at one point, they said they were sorry, but we would have to wait three or four weeks. When we asked why, they said because they had no newsprint. But we said, look at all the big advertising they had from Macy's and Gimbel's, and they said, yes, they had contracts. They told us to go to Macy's or Gimbel's and to tell them to waive a page, which was goodwill advertising anyway because they had sold everything. So we tried to find a contact at Macy's or Gimbel's, and Frances Gunther said she knew a man called Ira Hirschmann, the vice-president in charge of advertising, exactly the man we needed.[34]

So I met with Hirschmann to explain why the Emergency Committee was an important cause, and he called up the Times and waived some space of Bloomingdale's department store in favor of one of our ads. In the course of these conversations, he showed interest in the Committee's work and I suggested he become vice-president. Then I remember going to an executive committee meeting where Professor Smertenko[35] said he knew Hirschmann, "that he was no good." But for us the vice-president of Bloomingdale's was a big thing.

So he became a vice-president. We were working on sending a delegation of three people to Turkey to engage in actual [rescue] activities, but the State Department was blocking us all the way. We met with Secretary Cordell Hull and told him that one practical step would be to send a delegation to Turkey to open the doors. We said that the Jews of Europe were locked within, and that the United States government, the Allies, should help establish an area camp of twenty-five square miles in Turkey. We wanted to announce throughout Europe that Turkey would let in Jews, so that in Rumania, Hungary, or Germany or wherever there was a humane indi-

Ira Hirschmann, third from right, visiting Bergen-Belsen, the former Nazi concentration camp, in 1946.

vidual, or a crook who could be bribed, or just a good person who wanted to help a Jew escape, he would know that he could bring him to the border. Before that, a Jew arriving at a border couldn't get through, and people were afraid to help.

Well, at the State Department they told us they would take this suggestion under advisement. We had started early, but because we had no cooperation, everything was delayed. Every idea we had that could have been carried through with the power of American Jews behind it, was lost. So it took a year to put through an idea and it came out as a pigeon instead of an eagle. We chose Hirschmann to go to Turkey first.[36]

* * *

Q:[37] How did you end up going to Turkey?

HIRSCHMANN: Well, I began to investigate wherever possible the possibilities of rescue. I meanwhile became interested in forming or joining groups that were protesting. There was some mounting opposition, vocal but not effectual. I attended small meetings, and ones all the way up to the Madison Square Garden [rally] with Rabbi Stephen Wise and Einstein and others. After that, I decided that speaking would do nothing. We had to see if we could rescue some people. I was informed that there was a trickle of rescue, of escape in an underground out of Turkey which was the only country not in World War II at the time. I determined to get over there somehow so that I could rescue one person instead of all these speeches, the whole thing would be justified.

Q: And how did you get over there?

HIRSCHMANN: Well, I asked to go through the State Department and was blocked off by Breckinridge Long, Assistant Secretary of State in charge of refugees, who almost laughed me off. He said, "We're in the middle of a war, that goes much deeper than the involvement with Jews and we can't bother to get off the track." After that rebuff, I went back to my friends in the administration, around Roosevelt and started pushing; I felt that I should go. In the meanwhile, the information about the carnage, the destruction of Jews, had become more public and a group of vital, brilliant, and courageous young men around Henry Morgenthau, Jr., the Secretary of the Treasury, had pushed him to go to Roosevelt to establish an instrument which would give power to representatives to go to various parts of the world where Jews might be saved, or the remnants. That was what became the establishment of the War Refugee Board. . . . [Its] power included the appointment of representatives who had more power than the ambassadors in their countries. In fact, I did have ambassador authority. Because I had pressed to go to Turkey, I was appointed the first representative of the War Refugee Board for Turkey. With authority to act.

Q: Once you got there, what sort of problems did you find?

HIRSCHMANN: Well, the doors were locked, everybody was against—not me personally—but against my efforts. The newspaper men standing around the bar in Ankara laughed at me, said, "You're just wasting your time here." And the Turks had no interest in rescuing Jews; the British were opposed on principle, and they controlled all of the Middle East area; the boys in the American embassy thought I was an interloper, having come over their heads from Roosevelt; and all the other governments had no interest. One could easily have become discouraged.

I did find it was possible to bribe Turks. You could buy anything in Turkey, you could kill, buy the people to be killed and so forth. A group of young fellows from what was then Palestine had worked their way to Turkey in the hope of rescuing some Jews and bringing them into Palestine, and they were headed by Teddy Kollek who is now the mayor of Jerusalem, who was a young skinny guy in those days and I had put them to work—I had money available from America—to start getting shiploads of people out of Rumania. Thousands and thousands of Jews were incarcerated in a camp called Transnistria, which is now part of Russia, Bessarabia. And there were 150,000 originally. They were dying at the rate of a thousand a day. So I decided, I tried to work out some mechanism to break up that camp.

While I was in New York, preparing to go to Turkey, I met a number of Jewish leaders and I was put on to the former Rumanian ambassador to the United States. He defected from Rumania and stayed in the United States as a result of Hitler taking over Rumania. He gave me a letter to his friend Alexander Cretzianu, who was ambassador to Turkey, and he said, "You tell my friend Cretzianu he better get out of there—the Germans are going to lose and he's going to get trapped." I slipped the letter in my pocket and managed to hide it from the army boys who grabbed everything you had when you traveled, in spite of the fact that I had this important diplomatic passport, and decided some day I might use it.

While in Turkey, after I had seen there was no way of breaking through the Iron Guard who were controlling these thousands of people dying in Transnistria, I decided to get to Cretzianu if I could. A nice little fellow by the name of [Gilbert] Simond was acting as the representative to the International Red Cross and he made the rounds of the embassies in Ankara and which was a small kind of mountain country town, dotted with these little embassies on the same row. He used to make these rounds, and I said to him one day, "I have a letter to our enemy, that is the Rumanian ambassador, do you think you could bring him this letter, I'd like to meet him." And he said yes. It was a very risky business. And had I been caught dealing with the enemy in a private conversation, I think the game would have been up. I was being followed at every turn by the British intelligence, the Americans, the Turks, and the French. There's a law in America which forbids any American from dealing with the enemy during the war, which was called the Trading with the Enemy Act, it was started in the civil war, and Morgenthau and John Pehle, who was backing me all the time 100 percent, had taken the precaution before my leaving for Turkey to have that law [overridden] in my personal favor, which gave me more power than the regular ambassador.

So Simond thought this was great, and he immediately arranged a private meeting with Cretzianu and me out somewhere near his home in the suburbs, but we moved to a little wooded section in the hope that no one would be following us, for his very important meeting. We sat in a small room and each took out pencils. He was a very dapper good-looking man, spoke perfect English, talked and talked about nothing for some time, getting nowhere and I suddenly, in a rather undiplomatic way, turned around and said, "Mr. Ambassador, you're going to get killed, you and your family. He looked back, startled, and I said, "We've had military reports which you must have also, which indicate the Russians are on their way to Bessarabia and the first thing they'll do is get hold of you and Antonescu, the head of the Rumanian government, and they will take over Rumania." And he said, "So what?" And I said, "There's a way for you to be saved. There is a camp in Transnistria which is incarcerating—about 100,000 Jews are left. They're dying at the rate of a thousand a day, all you do is open that camp, and I will arrange to get you and your family a visa to the United States."

Well, I can only say that I had no more authority to do that than any remote person, to offer an enemy ambassador—at a time when we were bombing the oil fields in Rumania—to offer him a visa, was about as extreme a possibility as anybody could imagine. It came to me while I was sitting there, and also I wasn't so heroic about it. I just figured the chances of him accepting it were impossible. Well, he seemed very surprised and interested, and he said, "Well, what do we do?" And I said, "I want these people released and I'll get them out." He said, "What will we do with them, with 100,000 Jews?" And I said, "I'll take them, I'll get them out somehow. However, if you're at all interested, as a [demonstration] of your intention, I want 5,000 children delivered at the Port of Constanza," which faces on the Bosporus, where children could be moved to Istanbul.

I walked back out of the forest, to my hotel in Istanbul, and suddenly became aware of the reality of what I had done. In case he accepted, I had no authority whatever. If I made this report to my superiors in Washington, they not only would turn it down but fire me, for my acting without authority with the enemy. We could not put that report on the cryptograph because the Germans had broken our code—we knew it because we broke theirs in Ankara—however, this was a Saturday afternoon and on Monday, Simond came running to me in the embassy, saying, "He's back, he's seen [Prime Minister Ion] Antonescu, and he's ready to make the deal." Which was shocking to me because I had no authority, I was talking out of my head. I could not put anything on our cable to the effect that I'd dealt with the enemy, so I immediately asked to be flown back to Washington, which was not easy in wartime. This was a long trip, almost a week, around through North Africa, Casablanca, and through finally to cross the ocean. I had to get special authority to fly back, and arrived in Washington at the State Department full of trepidation.

And then happened one of these great pieces of fortune. A man by the name of Adolph Berle, who had worked with me on the La Guardia campaign, of which I had been chairman for a period, in the election of La Guardia to be mayor of New York in 1933, Adolph Berle had been the financial expert. He had been moved to Washington, where Roosevelt had used him in the State Department. He had been put on the refugee desk, as head of the refugee desk during my absence in Turkey and there I found my friend Berle sitting there, and he said, "What's the excitement, why did you have to get back here?" I said, "Well, I just made a deal, I need help, I've exchanged 100,000 people for four," and so forth. And I told him the story, and to my amazement and great relief, he said, "That's not bad at all, I think the President could back you up on that, as he called him the Skipper. He said, you stay out of this now, I'll go in and see him, and he did, and they agreed. And a visa was eventually arranged at the embassy in Ankara, and Cretzianu, his family could come to the U.S., which he did, he visited me in my office in New York. And 100,000 were released, many thousands did manage to come to Istanbul on the little boats, and then transport to what was then Palestine.

Q: What about the attitude of people like Pehle?

HIRSCHMANN: I had such overwhelming and overpowering support from John Pehle and his group in Washington, there's nothing I could say to overstate my great sense of gratification for their full-fledged support that I received. One time, I was sitting in my little office in Ankara . . . and the American ambassador [to Turkey, Laurence] Steinhardt, came down with a cable in his hands and said, "Otto, what are you doing tonight?," and I said, "Well, nothing, as usual, what do you think?" And he said, "Well, how about a game of cards, for some money?" I said, "What are you talking about?" And he said, "Well, gee, you don't know how much money you've got." I said, "What do you mean?" So he read to me from a cable to the effect that they were flying from Cairo two million gold sovereigns, which were 'for the personal use of Ira Hirschmann for his work in connection with his operations.' He said, "You'll be responsible for expenditures from these funds to me alone, John Pehle, as they are confidential funds from the Emergency Fund of the President of the United States, and may be dispersed without following any procedures usually required for government disbursements. If you encounter any obstacles, let me know immediately."

Now what Pehle did—I had indicated that I had to bribe Turks. I really bought these thousands of children who were saved on the boats, they weren't brought out, they were bought out. I had to pay them in gold sovereigns, and I had no receipts, I couldn't get receipts from Turkish pirates. And I sent messages back to the technical boys in the State Department and the government, and they said, "All right, we'll get you money but send us receipts for what you spend." Well, you can't get a receipt from a pirate. So I finally sent a message back after I was pressed for acknowledgment of the funds I was using, to the effect, "send anything back, a receipt, an account, a notation, or cross," and I sent a message back, "Any cross I would receive from the people with whom I'm dealing would be a double cross." That message got to Morgenthau and he took it and sent it to President Roosevelt. Pehle and his boys backed me in a way that to this very day I cannot speak about without fulsome gratitude.

∗   ∗   ∗

IV. Obstacles

DuBois and his colleagues encountered numerous obstacles from within the Roosevelt administration. In March 1944, they drafted a statement they wanted President Roosevelt to issue, warning the Germans against deporting Jews from newly occupied Hungary to the death camps. Presidential adviser and speechwriter Samuel Rosenman, a prominent member of the American Jewish Committee, persuaded FDR to delete three of the statement's six references to Jews, on the grounds that too much emphasis on Jews "would intensify anti-semitism in the United States." (See Appendix 3.)[38] In September 1944, the War Refugee Board staff prepared a statement they hoped would be issued by General Dwight Eisenhower, Supreme Commander of Allied forces in Europe, threatening punishment for anyone who collaborated in atrocities against Jews. At Eisenhower's insistence, the draft statement's reference to Jews was deleted. (See Appendix 4.)[39]

Likewise, DuBois and his colleagues soon discovered that senior State Department officials were unsympathetic to the War Refugee Board's rescue initiatives. In a meeting at the State Department in March, described by DuBois in the memorandum below, State officials objected to the board's plans to broadcast war crimes warnings through the U.S. government's Office of War Information and tried to pour cold water on the board's efforts to facilitate rescue via Spain.

What follows is an excerpt from a Memorandum for the Files by Josiah E. DuBois, Jr., March 2, 1944, describing a conference in the office of Undersecretary of State Edward Stettinius. The participants were Pehle and DuBois, representing

Elmer Davis, director of the Office of War Information, in the 1940s.

the War Refugee Board; Stettinius, Breckinridge Long, Adolph Berle, George Warren, Hayden Raynor, and Robert Pell, of the State Department; and Myron C. Taylor, representing the Intergovernmental Committee on Refugees:[40]

Myron Taylor started the conference by referring to the various agencies which are now in existence dealing with the refugee problem. He referred first to the President's Advisory Committee on Refugees. He then discussed the background of the Intergovernmental Committee. He called attention to the fact that at the suggestion of President Roosevelt an intergovernmental conference on the refugee problem was held at Evian in July 1938. Following this the original Intergovernmental Committee on Refugees was set up. . . . There followed the Bermuda Conference in 1943 after which the functions of the Intergovernmental Committee were broadened, etc. . . .

Pehle started by explaining some of the things which we have done to date. He discussed first the whole question of putting pressure on the satellite countries. He then began a discussion of our program through the O.W.I. designed to bring home to the persons in German controlled Europe the seriousness with which we view this matter and our determination to do what we can to save the Jews and other persecuted minorities from death.

At this point, Mr. Pell raised strong objections to any such propaganda program. He stated that State had cleared the O.W.I. directive which had been issued with "no comment" and at the present time the matter was at a standstill. There followed a brief discussion as to the desirability of this type of program. Mr. Pell took the point of view that the effect of such a propaganda program would be that the Germans would kill the Jews off faster rather than that the Germans would desist from their program of extermination. He stated that when he was in Germany he had talked with some of the Jewish leaders who had stressed the fact that we should not give any publicity to Germany's persecution of the Jews. Mr. Pehle indicated that he was in thorough disagreement with this point of view. There followed some further discussion during which Pehle and DuBois opposed Pell's point of view. . . .

Mr. Pehle then explained what we are trying to do in Spain. At this point Mr. Taylor raised the question as to the extent to which our Spanish program overlapped with what the IGC had been trying to do in Spain. He indicated that

[Intergovernmental Committee director Patrick] Malin had been scheduled to go to Spain. At this point Long interrupted and stated that the whole program of evacuation of refugees through Spain to North Africa had been undertaken outside of the IGC as a separate project. He also stated that Malin had never gone to Spain. There followed a brief debate between Mr. Taylor and Mr. Long as to what the IGC had done if anything in connection with the evacuation of refugees to and from Spain.

Pehle and DuBois stressed that the War Refugee Board was anxious to see the job done and was not anxious to take on any job that the IGC was in a better position to do. We stated that the Board is prepared to support the IGC in the execution of any projects which it has undertaken or proposes to undertake for the speedy evacuation of refugees and has no intention of interfering in the execution of such projects by the IGC. We stressed however that time is of the essence and that necessarily because of the way the IGC had been set up and was organized, it could not operate as speedily and effectively in many cases as the War Refugee Board.

By way of example, DuBois compared the handling of two particular cases, one by the War Refugee Board and one by the IGC. It was pointed out that the Board's representative in Turkey had cabled that it was possible to charter a Turkish ship provided that this Government could guarantee to the Turkish Government that this Government would replace the ship if lost. Within twenty-four hours the War Refugee Board had obtained the commitment of this Government to replace the ship. On the other side, there was a case in which in August of last year a cable was received from [U.S. diplomat Harold] Tittman in Rome indicating that the Italian Government was ready to supply ships to evacuate 30,000 Jews from the Rome area and requested immediate advice. After several weeks this matter was referred to the IGC on September 7. September 9 a cable was received from Winant stating that "having made an unsuccessful effort to convene a meeting of the Executive Committee (which apparently cannot meet before September 30) the Director of the Intergovernmental Committee on Refugees called an informal meeting in his office this afternoon at which the Embassy and Foreign Office were represented and the Director and Vice Director attended."

It was pointed out that this case was not cited to indicate that anything could necessarily have been done but to indicate that even in such an important matter as this it had been impossible to get even prompt consideration of the matter of the Executive Committee [of the IGC]. . . .

In connection with this whole matter Mr. Taylor raised the point as to where we intend to put refugees who have been evacuated. We asked Mr. Taylor what had been done about the suggestion made at the Bermuda Conference that the IGC take up with the British the possibility of using Tripolitania and Cyrenaica as havens of refuge. Mr. Taylor obviously did not know anything about this and referred the question to Mr. Long. Mr. Long replied that he had recently mentioned this matter to Sir Ronald Campbell [of the British Embassy in Washington] but that nothing as yet had been done about it. . . .

Mr. Pell then argued strongly that all approaches to other governments should be made through the IGC. Mr. Pehle said we would keep the IGC advised as to our activities. Mr. Taylor replied that keeping the IGC advised was not enough and that they should be consulted before acting.

J.E. DuBois, Jr.

*   *   *

Excerpt from a Memorandum for the Files by Josiah E. DuBois, Jr., May 26, 1944:[41]

Assistant Secretary of War [John J.] McCloy called me today concerning the refugee situation in Italy. He said that cables had just come in from Cairo indicating that the situation in Italy was getting very critical; that the refugees were arriving at the rate of 1800 a week; that the military authorities in Italy could not take care of them; that there were not sufficient facilities for putting these refugees up in Africa; and that something would have to be done to stop the flow of the refugees at least temporarily. McCloy added that it had been his understanding that we would only be getting refugees out in small numbers; that the rate at which they were now escaping was such that it was putting a real burden on General Wilson.

I told Mr. McCloy that it was my understanding that the difficulty was not one of transportation but one of finding havens of refuge to which these refugees could be taken. McCloy said that this was correct; that there was ample shipping; that the problem was finding places to put the refugees. I said that we have been working hard on this problem of finding havens of refuge. I asked him to send us the cables which had come in as soon as possible and said that we would look into the matter at once and get in touch with him. He said that he would immediately call General Hilldring and have him forward the cables to us.

Josiah E. DuBois, Jr.

*   *   *

DuBois:[42] [The problem of the] attitude of the British came to light again after the War Refugee Board was created—in 1944, just prior to the invasion of France, when it began to be clear that the Allies were probably going to win the war. And the Hungarians announced that they were willing to release [all Jewish children under ten who held visas to other countries, and all Jews with visas to Palestine]. Well, we attempted to get the British to go along with a joint statement that we would be willing to accept them, and the cables got nowhere.

Well, in the meantime, France was invaded. Secretary Morgenthau went over to London and France. The initial purpose was to look into the currency situation because the Treasury was handling the special currency that was used over there, but while we were over there we also discussed this particular cable. That is, Secretary Morgenthau discussed this particular offer by the Hungarians with the top people in the British government.

So finally, after he left, he left me behind to see what I could negotiate. As a result of his intervention, I saw Ambassador Winant personally. He was a very sympathetic man. And he made arrangements for his assistant . . . and myself, to go to see Undersecretary [George] Hall in the British [Foreign Office]. And we went to see him and presented this proposition, which he thought was incredulous. He couldn't believe that we would be willing to do that. And he gave the same—expressed the same attitude that was expressed in this cable that I read—"What are we going to do with them, Mr. DuBois, if they are released?"

So that when I said, "Well," I said, "I'm sure that I can get authority from my government to enter into a side agreement with you that if any Jews are released we will see to it that we find havens for them. I said the public declaration, for psychological reasons, should not even mention that side agreement. It should say that we, both governments, are willing.

He took that proposition and actually had a meeting of the British war cabinet and that's—he took it to [Foreign Minister Anthony] Eden, and Eden called a meeting of the British war cabinet, and they said yes, if the U.S. will do that, we will issue the joint statement.

I cabled back, of course, to Pehle and naturally I got back an answer, "Go ahead." And that's what happened, and I—we entered into such an agreement, which was confirmed by cable between the two governments, and then the public statement was made that the British and Americans would be willing to receive any Jews that the Hungarians would release, and of course that was broadcast all over Europe in the underground radio and so forth. How much good that did psychologically, I mean, you don't know—but at least it was better than saying "no."

*   *   *

In April 1944, Rudolf Vrba and Alfred Wetzler escaped from Auschwitz.[43] After an eleven-day, eighty-mile trek through southern Poland, Vrba and Wetzler reached Slovakia, where they met with Jewish leaders and dictated a thirty-page report that came to be known as the Auschwitz Protocols. It included details of the mass-murder process, maps pinpointing the gas chambers and crematoria, and warnings of the impending slaughter of Hungary's Jews. Jewish leaders in Bratislava delivered the report to foreign diplomats and it reached the British Foreign Office in late July. "Even if one allows for customary Jewish exaggeration, these stories are frightful," one official grudgingly conceded in a note written in the margin.

Another copy of Vrba's Auschwitz Protocols was given to Rabbi Michoel Dov Weissmandel, a rescue activist in Bratislava, who then wrote the first known appeal for the use of Allied air power to disrupt the mass murder. Weissmandel's plea to the Allies to bomb the railroad lines between Hungary and Auschwitz reached the Roosevelt administration in June.

The protocols were forwarded by the Jewish Agency representative in Geneva, Richard Lichtheim, to the Agency leadership in Jerusalem. Agency leaders had initially opposed bombing Auschwitz because they believed it was a labor camp, not *a death camp. But after receiving the Auschwitz Protocols in June, Agency leaders and emissaries lobbied British, American, and Soviet officials to bomb the camp or the railways leading to it. Their requests were rebuffed.*

A condensed version of the Auschwitz Protocols had reached the War Refugee Board in June and helped galvanize the Board to mobilize international pressure on Hungary to halt the deportations to Auschwitz. The full version reached the Board in October, setting off the controversy described below.[44]

*   *   *

PEHLE:[45] We received from two people who had escaped from Auschwitz detailed stories of how the extermination camps worked. And we released this to the press with a one-week release date. And I got a call from Elmer Davis who was a liberal correspondent who was head of the Office of War Information, asking me to cancel the press release, which of course I couldn't do. And asking me to come down to his office and to talk, and all these people agreed that it should be canceled too because no one would believe it. And people would doubt it. And they would think the government was issuing false information.

Which I mention just because it shows the unwillingness to accept the horrible facts about what was going on. And of course we didn't call it back and it received front-page coverage in the *New York Times* and also in some other newspapers.

*   *   *

Excerpt from a memorandum for the files by Virginia M. Mannon of the War Refugee Board, November 22, 1944, regarding "Mr. Elmer Davis' questioning of War Refugee Board's release of German atrocity stories":[46]

At Mr. Davis' request Mr. Pehle went to see Mr. Davis in his office at the Social Security Building a 2:30 pm today. Accompanying Mr. Pehle were [two of his assistants].

Mr. Davis had with him [six] members of his staff. . . .

Over the telephone Mr. Davis had raised some objections to the War Refugee Board's issuing a press release on the German atrocity stories which had been mailed to the press Saturday, November 18 for release Sunday, November 26. He had asked Mr. Pehle to come to his office to discuss the subject further.

Background: A summary of the reports had been sent to the Board in July by Roswell McClelland, Board representative in Switzerland. The full reports had been sent to the Board by Mr. McClelland in October via diplomatic pouch. The Board decided to release the reports to the press and did so without clearing them with OWI. Failure to clear with OWI was unintentional; the Board was unaware that in 1942 Mr. Davis had issued an order saying that news releases "relating significantly to the war effort" must be cleared and issued by OWI. . . .

Discussion in Mr. Davis' Office: Mr. Davis led off by asking Mr. Pehle the source of the reports. Mr. Pehle read excerpts of Mr. McClelland's covering letter vouching for their authenticity. Mr. Davis' staff unanimously viewed with alarm the War Refugee Board's release of the reports. Their reasons were various. Mr.

Davis called on each of his staff members to express himself. They thought there would be a bad reaction overseas. They pointed out that they would have to give the stories some overseas play, since the press associations here would undoubtedly carry them. They brought up the question of the stories being concerned with a multiplicity of "mean little things," the idea of seeming to condemn war criminals by issuing a release with a heading "Executive Office of the President," the Army and Navy's decision not to issue Jap atrocity stories because of reprisals on American prisoners, the question of whether the reports had not been planted by anti-Semites (because of the reference to Jews being cruel to Jews), the inadvisability of timing such a release one week after the opening of the Sixth War Loan, etc. [One OWI staff member] asked Mr. Pehle what his purpose was in releasing the reports. Then Mr. Davis read a news item from Reuters off the ticker which, apparently, was a piece of German propaganda saying that American Jewish officers were treating German prisoners of war in much the manner Jewish refugees were treated by the Germans. They all expressed fear of the reaction to the reports, but when asked by Mr. Pehle if they expected a bad press reaction, said no. In fact, Mr. Dood admitted he expected favorable editorials and they would use them overseas.

The whole meeting was pretty futile, since the release was a fait accompli. Mr. Davis said Army, State, and OSS had refused to clear the reports because they were already released. Mr. Davis asked what distribution had been made and said another order had been flouted when he was told that the stories were sent to editors all over the country. He said the releases should have gone only to Washington bureaus. The enormity of the crimes which the WRB had perpetrated against the OWI was so great that Mr. Davis admitted there was practically nothing to be done at this late date. He suggested the possibility of the Board's issuing an additional statement to all recipients of the release pointing out that the reports came via an agent of the WRB who had taken precautions to ensure their authenticity. Mr. Pehle said he would consider it.

Mr. Pehle demolished their objections one by one, explaining that he had talked with Congressman Celler, representatives of Jewish organizations in New York and Secretary Morgenthau, that none of them had felt any fears such as those voiced by OWI. He reminded them that OWI had widely publicized the President's statement of March 24, the statements of the House Foreign Affairs Committee and Senate Foreign Relations Committee and the statement by Archbishop Spellman[47] which had the same purpose as these reports. He also pointed out that there was considerable doubt in many people's minds as to whether anything actually was going to be done about war criminals. When asked if this were the WRB's first atrocity report, Mr. Pehle said yes, and it would doubtless be the last.

At least three times Mr. Davis said the head of his Polish desk had read the reports carefully and had stated that the events in the reports might well have happened.

* * *

Excerpts from a letter by Elmer Davis, director of the Office of War Information, to John Pehle, director of the War Refugee Board, November 23, 1944:[48]

Dear Mr. Pehle:

... [M]y attention has been called (subsequent to yesterday's meeting) to the fact that the two Slovak refugees [who authored the Auschwitz Protocols] quoted had been block recorders at Birkenau; which suggests the possibility that their escape might have been arranged or facilitated by the German authorities. Such a suspicion may be quite unjust; but the fact remains that several readers in this office felt that the story would create contempt for the inmates (whether Jewish or Aryan) of concentration camps; and it would not be beyond the German Propaganda Ministry to try to create that impression, even at the cost of including materials about atrocities committed by Germans. They know that their own record is well known here, and might feel that the best they can do is to try to smear other nationalities on the same count. ...

Cordially,

Elmer Davis

Director

* * *

The OWI's attitude reflected the perspective that had prevailed in administration policymaking at least until the spring of 1944. U.S. officials feared that calling attention to the fact that the Jews were being singled out for persecution would increase pressure on the United States to grant them refuge. Thus a meeting of the American, British, and Soviet foreign ministers in Moscow in October 1943 had issued a statement threatening postwar punishment for Nazi war crimes against conquered populations. It mentioned "French, Dutch, Belgian or Norwegian hostages ... Cretan peasants ... the people of Poland"—but not Jews. Even FDR's 1944 message commemorating the first anniversary of the Warsaw Ghetto revolt did not mention the Jews. Arthur Szyk, the famous artist and Jewish rescue activist, remarked bitterly that Europe's Jews were being "treat[ed] as a pornographical subject—you cannot discuss it in polite society."[49]

V. Haven in Oswego

DuBois:[50] Another incident that I was personally involved in was, I made the recommendation to John Pehle who passed it on to Secretary Morgenthau that it would be better to treat the Jews as prisoners of war than to let them die, and I suggested that we set up prisoner of war camps in the United States in which we could bring these people, keep them there, and then send them back after the war is over. In the meantime, treat them as prisoners of war.

I prepared a memorandum on that. Secretary Morgenthau took the idea to President Roosevelt, who magnanimously—I say that with some sarcasm—agreed to set up such a haven in the United States.

Now, he picked out an army camp, an abandoned army camp in Oswego [New York] which would take 1,000 persons and that was the result of that program. We did receive 1,000 people, but to me although it had a psychological impact it was far, far below what this government should have done. There's no reason why we shouldn't have made an offer that we'll house anybody here that you're willing to let out.

*   *   *

A memorandum to President Roosevelt, drafted by Josiah E. DuBois, Jr., in March 1944, urging temporary refuge in the United States for Jews fleeing Hitler:[51]

Memorandum for the President

In the Executive Order creating the War Refugee Board you directed that the Board make appropriate recommendations to you to overcome any difficulties encountered in the rescue and relief of war refugees.

Although the Board has already initiated many measures which, if fully implemented, may result in saving the lives of refugees, there is one basic obstacle which lies athwart all our efforts. This is the simple fact that the United Nations have not been prepared to supply even temporary havens of refuge for substantial numbers of the persecuted peoples of Europe, particularly the Jews.

Why This Is the Main Obstacle

The following brief summary will reveal why this constitutes the basic weakness in our whole program.

(1) Our best chance of saving many people from death, particularly after recent events in the Balkans, lies in an effort to convince the Hitlerite forces, and more particularly their functionaries and subordinates, that it is in their interest to spare the lives of these people. In this connection, the statement issued by you on March 24, which is being given the widest possible publicity in German controlled territory, will of course be most helpful toward this end, especially if followed by concrete action.

(2) And there is also an opportunity to actually bring some of these people out of enemy territory. The recent developments in the Balkans limit opportunities there, but there still remains a possibility of stimulating the flow of refugees to Spain and Switzerland.

(3) It is essential to both of these avenues of approach, however, that we and our allies convince the world of our sincerity and our willingness to bear our share of the burden. Thus, great substance would be added to our threats, and other countries would be much more ready to cooperate in aiding the escape of refugees, if we made it clear now by action that our doors are open to these people.

(4) The United Nations must not merely threaten our enemies and ask them to stop killing Jews; the United Nations must offer to take the Jews themselves. Only in that way can the great moral issue involved be made clear.

Such a step would show the Germans clearly that our threats of punishment and promises of action are not mere words. It is even possible that after such an announcement the Germans might be prepared to release or permit the escape of these persecuted peoples.

(5) And such a step would certainly cause the neutral countries to encourage the entry of more refugees into their territory since they would then know that they would not be required to keep all refugees until the war ends. Thus, one of the reasons why we are not meeting with any success in Spain is the fact that the Spaniards are not convinced that we will take the refugees off their hands. Although we have been stating for a long while that we are going to take the Jewish refugees in Spain to a small camp in North Africa, none have been moved there to date. This has been due primarily to the reluctant attitude of the French. And the inarticulate major premise of the French attitude undoubtedly is the conviction that such refugees are to be dumped and left in French Africa and that neither the United States nor Great Britain will receive them.

Proposed Solution

John W. Pehle has strongly recommended that this Government act at once in this humanitarian cause and announce to the world that we will provide temporary havens of refuge in this country for all oppressed peoples escaping from Hitler—these people to be placed in camps established in this country and to remain there until the termination of the war at which time they will be returned to their homelands.

Nature and Benefits of Proposal

(1) Under this proposal the refugees would be treated in effect as prisoners of war. They would be brought into the country outside the regular immigration procedure just as civilian internees from Latin American countries have been brought here and placed in internment camps. No violation or attempt to evade immigration laws would be involved since the refugees would remain only until the termination of the war and would not come in under the quota system. There could be no objection on security grounds any more than in the case of prisoners of war.

(2) The principal United Nations involved have already agreed that each of them will receive after the war its nationals who have fled for their lives and have been given asylum in other countries. These nations have also agreed that it is a part of their settled policy to assure such conditions in enemy and enemy occupied territories as will permit the return thereto of all persons displaced therefrom who have sought refuge elsewhere. This agreement, already concurred in by the United States, Great Britain, the Soviet Union, Luxembourg, Yugoslavia, Norway, the French Committee, Greece, Belgium, Poland, Czechoslovakia, and the Netherlands should serve to make clear to those concerned that such refugees as may be accepted in camps here will be returned to their homelands at the end of the war.

(3) The humanitarian considerations which might be urged against the confinement of the refugees are answered by the simple fact that treating them as prisoners of war is better than letting them die.

(4) The general idea has been discussed with a number of organizations, Jewish and non-Jewish, and they have all expressed their approval. Most of them feel that it is by far the biggest step the Board can take to accomplish the purposes for which it was established.

(5) The necessity for unilateral action now by this Government lies in the fact that we cannot expect others to do what we ourselves will not do, and if we are to act in time we must take the lead.

(6) The practical effect of such a step by the United States might be tremendous. Our allies would without doubt follow our lead. That this country, which has always been a refuge for the fugitive from injustice, oppression and persecution, should take the leadership in this matter would be in keeping with our heritage and with our ideals of liberty and justice.

(7) In the hearts and minds of all peoples under Nazi domination and throughout the world such action might well have an effect very much favorable to our whole war effort and to our reputation as a nation which has always carried the torch in great undertakings.

(8) Even if no refugees were ever actually brought to these camps, the mere announcement of our readiness to receive them would remove the basic obstacle to our efforts to save them. In view of geographical and time factors, it is not likely that many refugees would actually come to the United States. The important thing is that we offer to receive them.

Risks of Proposal

The following risks involved in this proposal must be weighed against the humanitarian and other considerations mentioned above:

(1) The danger that such a program would result in a breakdown of our immigration laws. The point made is that no matter what we say now about these people returning to their homes when the war is over, they will not want to return, and that an almost irresistible pressure will be created on Congress to change the law and allow such people to remain in this country.

(2) The danger that it would provoke unfavorable public reaction and would give anti-Semitic and other groups as well as certain elements in Congress an opportunity to attack you and the Board.

Recommendation of the Board

Secretary Hull, Secretary Morgenthau and Secretary Stimson carefully considered this proposal at the meeting of the Board on March 21. Although there was no disagreement as to the potential benefits of such a program, Secretary Stimson felt that the risks involved outweighed the benefits. It was decided that in view of the importance and urgency of this matter and the great responsibility involved in making a decision, it should be submitted to you for your consideration.

In your consideration of how this matter could be presented to the public, you may wish to examine the attached draft of a statement which might be issued by you.

We would appreciate an early expression of your views.

Secretary of State.

Secretary of the Treasury.

Secretary of War.

*   *   *

Excerpts from a meeting between Morgenthau, Pehle, and DuBois, May 1, 1944:[52]

MR. DuBois: [T]his whole issue depends on whether or not you are behind this enough to really fight for it. I have the feeling that you are probably not.

H.M.JR: That is correct.

MR. DuBois: Now, my own feeling is the thing doesn't have a chance as long as you feel that way about it, to be very frank with you. I think it is fair to say that we feel that this thing is not only important from the refugee standpoint, it is the most important step that you could take in the refugee field, but I think it is also an important step from many points of view.

H.M.JR: I don't see it.

MR. DuBois: From the psychological warfare point of view, and everything else. I don't think—we just found a couple of days ago that the AF of L passed a resolution—last September, wasn't it?

MR. PEHLE: That is right.

MR. DuBois: . . . recommending this very same thing, in substance. Many organizations have written in to us.

H.M.JR: I don't want to be in the position of jockeying. I am perfectly willing to go [to Hull for his signature].

MR. PEHLE: We are not trying jockey . . . All right. But if you have doubts about this thing, I would like to know what they are.

H.M.JR: No, I just don't want to be out on the front on it.

MR. DuBois: Is it, Mr. Secretary, that you are not sold on the wisdom of this from the refugee standpoint, that you feel it isn't the time to do it?

H.M.JR: No, I just don't think you can get it through Congress.

MR. PEHLE: What we are shooting for is not to go through Congress.

H.M.JR: Well, the President shouldn't do it, then. He shouldn't get Congress down on him. . . .

MR. DuBois: I have always thought strongly you should do it without going to Congress.

H.M.JR: Well, I don't.

MR. PEHLE: Then, frankly, Mr. Secretary, I don't think it represents a fair statement of your views. If you feel that way—I disagree strongly with that, myself.

H.M.Jr: That is your privilege.

Mr. Pehle: The more I have been with this issue, and the more there has been publicity on it, the more support we have gotten. We haven't gotten any blasts.

H.M.Jr: I still say I don't think the President should take this on. You certainly should consult the [congressional] leaders.

Mr. Pehle: Oh, that is something else.

H.M.Jr: . . . I think, from all the evidence of Congress, that if he did this thing, that they could get a resolution through countermanding any Executive Order.

Mr. DuBois: I don't believe it.

Mr. Pehle: Not today, in view of the elections. . . .

The process by which DuBois's havens proposals advanced, despite Secretary Morgenthau's initial misgivings, is described in Chapter 6.

VI. Proposals to Bomb Auschwitz

McClelland:[53] The most dramatic example of how we could use transmission . . . of information was that of the first authentic report [by Vrba and Wetzler] on the whole Auschwitz-Birkenau extermination complex that arrived in Geneva, actually through Czech underground channels . . . in June 1944 . . . Agudath Israel, Sternbuch's organization,[54] were the ones that made the suggestion . . . to bomb the railways [leading to Auschwitz]. . . . But of course, it couldn't have been made until you had some concrete idea of what sort of an installation was involved and where it went. . . . [So] I made whatever efforts I could to take this report . . . and to check out the specific elements, in particular the exact geographic location of this establishment.

I can recall finding a man in Geneva who had done the large-scale maps of Upper Silesia, I believe, for the League of Nations—getting the map so we could try to pinpoint as accurately as possible just where the Auschwitz and Birkenau installations were located. In that connection, since this terrible installation was working night and day the suggestion was made, and I think for the first time to me by Dr. Sternbuch, the Union of Orthodox Rabbis, and possibly Gerhardt Riegner, who was familiar with the original report, that an effort might be made to bomb the rail lines leading to Auschwitz as one means of at least temporarily halting this massive deportation of Jews from Hungary. Once that recommendation had been sent to Washington it was pretty well out of my hands, so there was nothing that I could do to directly influence it. It was, as we know later, considered at some length in Washington by the military and rejected as prejudicial to the war effort or impractical—that remains somewhat of a moot point in the light of information that has come up later, the bombing that was being done against the I.G. Farben artificial rubber plant at Birkenau [a few miles from the gas chambers].

* * *

Letter from Assistant Secretary of War John J. McCloy to John Pehle, July 4, 1944:[55]

Dear Mr. Pehle:

I refer to your letter of June 29, inclosing [*sic*] a cable from your representative in Bern, Switzerland, proposing that certain sections of railway lines between Hungary and Poland be bombed to interrupt the transportation of Jews from Hungary.

The War Department is of the opinion that the suggested air operation is impracticable. It could be executed only by the diversion of considerable air support essential to the success of our forces now engaged in decisive operations and would in any case be of such very doubtful efficacy that it would not amount to a practical project.

The War Department fully appreciates the humanitarian motives which prompted the suggested operation but for the reasons stated above the operation suggested does not appear justified.

Sincerely,

John J. McCloy

* * *

The tragic irony of McCloy's "diversion" argument is that the Roosevelt administration did divert resources and alter military plans because of nonmilitary considerations on various occasions—just not for Jews. General Patton diverted his Second Cavalry to rescue the prized Lipizzaner dancing horses, which were being held prisoner by the Germans at a site near the Czech–Austrian border. A U.S. Air Force plan to bomb the Japanese city of Kyoto was blocked by Secretary of War Henry Stimson because of the city's artistic treasures. Assistant Secretary of War John McCloy was moved to divert bombers from striking the German city of Rothenburg because of its famous medieval architecture. FDR ordered airdrops of supplies to the Polish Home Army rebels in Warsaw even though his advisers warned him it would tie up large numbers of planes and most of the supplies would be confiscated by the Germans.

Assistant Secretary of War John J. McCloy.

In 1943, the State Department, which opposed any U.S. government action to rescue Jews from Hitler, did establish its own rescue agency—a government commission "for the protection and salvage of artistic and historic monuments in Europe."

The real problem was that the Allies did not want to have tens of thousands of Jewish refugees on their hands. Roosevelt did not want to bring more refugees to America. England did not want more Jews going to Mandatory Palestine.

The Zionist leader Rabbi Meyer Berlin was tragically prescient when he remarked to

U.S. Senator Robert Wagner in early 1943: "If horses were being slaughtered as are the Jews of Poland, there would by now be a loud demand for organized action against such cruelty to animals. Somehow, when it concerns Jews, everybody remains silent."[56]

* * *

PEHLE:[57] After we made the recommendation to Assistant Secretary McCloy that the extermination facilities of Auschwitz be bombed, we were told that this was not possible. When we pursued this further, we were told that this would involve bombers being sent from England and that fighters could not escort bombers that far and therefore it was not possible to do this.

Later, perhaps after the war, we discovered that at the very time that we were recommending this, bombing all around Auschwitz was going on from Italy. And we had been misled.

In 1944, George S. McGovern, the future U.S. Senator and 1972 Democratic presidential nominee, was the pilot of a B-24 Liberator plane in the 455th Bomb Group stationed in Allied-liberated Italy. On December 26, 1944, McGovern's squadron dropped fifty tons of bombs on the oil plants at Monowitz, an industrial section of Auschwitz. A few stray bombs accidentally struck an SS sick bay and killed five SS men.

"There is no question we should have attempted . . . to go after Auschwitz," McGovern said in a postwar interview. "There was a pretty good chance we could have blasted those rail lines off the face of the earth, which would have interrupted the flow of people to those death chambers, and we had a pretty good chance of knocking out those gas ovens." The War Department's claim that bombing Auschwitz would mean "diverting" military resources from more urgent operations was just "a rationalization," according to McGovern. "Franklin Roosevelt was a great man and he was my political hero," McGovern said. "But I think he made two great mistakes in World War II." One was the internment of Japanese-Americans; the other was the decision "not to go after Auschwitz. . . . God forgive us for that tragic miscalculation."

McGovern acknowledged the danger that some prisoners might be harmed by such bombing. Nonetheless, he contended in the interview, "it was certainly worth the effort, despite all the risks," because the prisoners were already "doomed to death" and an Allied bombing attack "could have disrupted the slaughter," thus saving many more lives.[58] *Auschwitz inmates themselves prayed for the camp to be bombed, even though they might have been killed in the process. Elie Wiesel, in his book* Night *(1960), described a U.S. bombing raid near Auschwitz that he witnessed as a teenager when he was assigned to a slave labor battalion outside the main camp: "[I]f a bomb had fallen on the blocks [the prisoners' barracks], it alone would have claimed hundreds of victims on the spot. But we were no longer afraid of death; at any rate, not of that death. Every bomb that exploded filled us with joy and gave us new confidence in life. The raid lasted over an hour. If it could only have lasted ten times ten hours!"*[59]

* * *

Excerpts from a memorandum by War Refugee Board staff member Benjamin Akzin to his colleague Lawrence Lesser, June 29, 1944:[60]

By Cable No. 4041 of June 21, from Bern, McClelland, reporting on the deportation and extermination of Hungarian Jews, states that "there is little doubt that many of these Hungarian Jews are being sent to the extermination camps of AUSCHWITZ (OSWIECIM) and BIRKENAU (RAJSKA) in Western Upper Silesia where according to recent reports, since early summer 1942 at least 1,500,000 Jews have been killed. There is evidence that already in January 1944 preparations were being made to receive and exterminate Hungarian Jews in these camps."

In view of the preeminent part evidently played by these two extermination camps in the massacre of Jews, equipped to kill 125,000 people per month, it would seem that the destruction of their physical installations might appreciably slow down the systematic slaughter at least temporarily. The methodical German mind might require some time to rebuild the installations or to evolve elsewhere equally efficient procedures of mass slaughter and of disposing of the bodies. Some saving of lives would therefore be a most likely result of the destruction of the two extermination camps.

Though no exaggerated hopes should be entertained, this saving of lives might even be quite appreciable, since, in the present stage of the war, with German manpower and material resources gravely depleted, German authorities might not be in a position to devote themselves to the task of equipping new large-scale extermination centers.

Aside from the preventive significance of the destruction of the two camps, it would also seem correct to mark them for destruction as a matter of principle, as the most tangible—and perhaps only tangible—evidence of the indignation aroused by the existence of these charnel-houses. It will also be noted that the destruction of the extermination camps would presumably cause many deaths among their personnel—certainly among the most ruthless and despicable of the Nazis.

It is suggested that the foregoing be brought to the attention of the appropriate political and military authorities, with a view to considering the feasibility of a thorough destruction of the two camps by aerial bombardment. It may be of interest, in this connection, that the two camps are situated in the industrial region of Upper Silesia, near the important mining and manufacturing centers of Katowice and Chorzow (Oswiecim lies about 14 miles southeast of Katowice), which play an important part in the industrial armament of Germany. Therefore, the destruction of these camps could be achieved without deflecting aerial strength from an important zone of military objectives.

Presumably, a large number of Jews in these camps may be killed in the course of such bombings (though some of them may escape in the confusion). But such Jews are doomed to death anyhow. The destruction of the camps would not change their fate, but it would serve as visible retribution on their murderers and it might save the lives of future victims.

It will be noted that the inevitable fate of Jews herded in ghettoes near the industrial and railroad installations in Hungary has not caused the United Nations to stop bombing these installations. It is submitted, therefore, that refraining from bombing the extermination centers would be sheer misplaced sentimentality, far more cruel than a decision to destroy these centers.

B.A.

* * *

GOODWIN:[61] Joe [DuBois] told me that he and his colleagues tried to convince the War Department to bomb the railway lines leading to Auschwitz. But he said the military replied that they couldn't "waste bombs on nonmilitary targets." He found that kind of thinking very frustrating.

* * *

Letter from Assistant Secretary of War John J. McCloy to A. Leon Kubowitzki, chief of the Rescue Department of the World Jewish Congress, August 14, 1944:[62]

Dear Mr. Kubowitzki:

I refer to your letter of August 9 in which you request consideration of a proposal made by Mr. Ernest Frischer that certain installations and railroad centers be bombed.

The War Department has been approached by the War Refugee Board, which raised the question of the practicability of this suggestion. After a study it became apparent that such an operation could be executed only by the diversion of considerable air support essential to the success of our forces now engaged in decisive operations elsewhere and would in any case be of such doubtful efficacy that it would not warrant the use of our resources. There has been considerable opinion to the effect that such an effort, even if practicable, might provoke even more vindictive action by the Germans.

The War Department fully appreciates the humanitarian motives which prompted the suggested operation, but for the reasons stated above it has not been felt that it can or should be undertaken, at least at this time.

Sincerely,
John J. McCloy
Assistant Secretary of War

* * *

Letter from John Pehle, director of the War Refugee Board, to Assistant Secretary of War John J. McCloy, November 8, 1944:[63]

Dear Mr. McCloy:

I send you herewith copies of two eyewitness descriptions of the notorious German concentration and extermination camps of Auschwitz and Birkenau in Upper Silesia, which have just been received from the Board's Special Representative in Bern, Switzerland, Roswell McClelland whom we have borrowed from the American Friends Service Committee. No report of Nazi atrocities received by the Board has quite caught the gruesome brutality of what is taking place in these camps of horror as have these sober, factual accounts of conditions in Auschwitz and Birkenau. I earnestly hope that you will read these reports.

The destruction of large numbers of people apparently is not a simple process. The Germans have been forced to devote considerable technological ingenuity and administrative know-how in order to carry out murder on a mass production basis, as the attached reports will testify. If the elaborate murder installations at Birkenau were destroyed, it seems clear that the Germans could not reconstruct them for some time.

Until now, despite pressure from many sources, I have been hesitant to urge the destruction of these camps by direct, military action. But I am convinced that the point has now been reached where such action is justifiable if it is deemed feasible by competent military authorities. I strongly recommend that the War Department give serious consideration to the possibility of destroying the execution chambers and crematories in Birkenau through direct bombing action. It may be observed that there would be other advantages of a military nature to such an attack. The Krupp and Siemens factories, where among other things cases for hand grenades are made, and a Buna plant, all within Auschwitz, would be destroyed. The destruction of the German barracks and guardhouses and the killing of German soldiers in the area would also be accomplished. The morale of underground groups might be considerably strengthened by such a dramatic exhibition of Allied air support and a number of the people confined in Auschwitz and Birkenau might be liberated in the confusion resulting from the bombing. That the effecting of a prison break by such methods is not without precedent is indicated by the description in the enclosed copy of a recent *New York Times* article of the liberation from Amiens prison of 100 French patriots by the RAF.

Obviously, the War Refugee Board is in no position to determine whether the foregoing proposal is feasible from a military standpoint. Nevertheless in view of the urgency of the situation, we feel justified in making the suggestion. I would appreciate having the view of the War Department as soon as possible.

Very truly yours,
J.W. Pehle
Executive Director

VII. Defining War Crimes

Excerpts from a Memorandum for the Files by Josiah E. DuBois, Jr., August 17, 1944:[64]

Following are the highlights of my conference today with Herbert Pell, American member on the United Nations Commission for the Investigation of War Crimes:

1. Mr. Pell said that he wanted to give me some information concerning the Commission which has not been made public, but which I could feel free to pass on to the War Refugee Board. . . .

Mr. Pell then went on to explain that his Commission did not have jurisdiction over many of the crimes which the Nazi[s] were perpetuating. Thus, for example, he stated that the Commission had taken the point of view that "war crimes" must be established in accordance with the definition of "war crimes" as used in international law and that it only relates to crimes committed by one belligerent against another belligerent (or its citizens) and sometimes crimes committed by a nation against its own subjects or by a nation against the subjects of one of its Allies. Applying this to the case of the persecution and annihilation of minorities in occupied Europe, crimes as the Commission defined it would include crimes committed against Polish citizens by Germans, but would not include acts against German citizens by Germans, Hungarian citizens against Hungary, etc., or the crimes by Germans against Hungarian citizens, Rumanian citizens, etc.

I told Mr. Pell that whatever the definition of "war crimes" may have been in the past, to make the distinction he was talking about in the light of the realities of the present war did not make sense to me, and that many of the concepts developed in international law had to be revised in the light of the facts of the present war; that merely because war crimes may have been defined in such a narrow sense in relation to past wars should not be used as a necessary precedent in relation to the present war.

Mr. Pell said that he agreed with this point of view but that other members of the Commission (most of whom were lawyers—Mr. Pell not being a lawyer) disagreed and took the position that they were bound by the concept of war crime which had already been accepted in international law.

Mr. Pell said that he felt that crimes such as the crimes by Germany against its own citizens and citizens of Hungary should be brought within the jurisdiction of his Commission. He said that he felt that the best way of tackling this problem was not by trying to convince the members that the definition of war crimes should be broadened but rather that each country should instruct its representatives on the Commission that these particular crimes should be dealt with by the Commission. Specifically he suggested that if the United States Government should instruct him to this effect he felt that this would go a long way towards getting this position adopted. Pell further suggested the possibility of having it appear in the press of the United States that the United States Government had so instructed its member. . . .

Pell said that he thought that most of the United Nations in Europe would actually punish war criminals but that the United States and Great Britain would probably be very soft hearted about the matter. . . .

Pell made it clear that he hoped that I would take up the matter of the scope of the jurisdiction of his Commission over "war crimes" in Washington. He specifically mentioned that it might be brought to the attention of Secretary Hull and reiterated that if he could get the proper instructions from Washington he could carry on from there.

J.E. DuBois, Jr.

Herbert Pell, 1948.

* * *

Excerpts from a memorandum from War Refugee Board Director John Pehle to Undersecretary of State Edward Stettinius, August 28, 1944:[65]

As you know, a major activity of the War Refugee Board has been psychological warfare designed to induce and persuade the enemy to cease the persecution of the Jews and other minorities. The basis of this program, which has been carried out in cooperation with the State Department, Office of War Information and other agencies, has been the threat to punish every Axis war criminal who has participated, directly or indirectly, in such persecution. Threats of this nature had been made by the United Nations, including various branches of this Government, even before the War Refugee Board was established, and they have since been repeated with increasing tempo. . . .

We had assumed that one of the primary functions of the United Nations Commission for the Investigation of War Crimes which was created in 1943, would be to devise procedures for the gathering of evidence and the ascertainment, trial and punishment of those enemy nationals who had participated in such war crimes. Much to our surprise we were informed by our General Counsel, Mr. Josiah E. DuBois, upon his return from London recently that he understood from a conversation with Mr. Pell, the United States representative on the Commission, that the Commission takes the view that war crimes under international law do not include crimes committed by an Axis nation or its nationals against its own subjects of another Axis nation. Accordingly, it appears that the Commission is not making any provision for the just punishment of such war criminals.

Needless to say, it would be a fearful miscarriage of justice if such war criminals were permitted to escape punishment for their inhuman crimes. Moreover, the failure to implement the numerous threats of punishment would not only subject to ridicule the authors thereof, but would render it far more difficult to deter similar criminal conduct in the future. The failure to punish the criminals of World War I may well have removed a deterrent to the commission of brutalities against civilian populations in this war, including the mass murder of the Jews.

According to Mr. DuBois' report, Mr. Pell is not satisfied with this position of the United Nations Commission for the Investigation of War Crimes, but seems not to have received instructions from this Government in the matter. Mr.

Pell believes that the most effective way of inducing the Commission to broaden the scope of its work to include the punishment of all Axis war criminals, including those guilty of crimes against persons in the above categories, would be to have the United States Government instruct him to urge the Commission to include such crimes in its program and, if possible, to have the other governments represented on the Commission instruct their representatives along similar lines. Another suggested step would be to publicize such an instruction by releasing it to the press.

Accordingly, we suggest that the Department advise Mr. Pell along the lines of the proposed cable attached hereto indicating clearly that the declared policy of the United States Government is to ensure the just punishment of all Axis War criminals, including those guilty of crimes against the Jews and other minorities whether or not the victims of such crimes are of the same nationality as the evildoers; and that Mr. Pell should insist upon the formulation of a program by the Commission effectuating this policy.

J.W. Pehle
Executive Director

* * *

Excerpts from a letter by the War Refugee Board's representative in London, James Mann, to WRB director John Pehle, September 19, 1944:[66]

Dear John:

. . . I have talked with Herbert Pell, American member of the War Crimes Commission, and he has not yet received any instructions from Washington along the lines of the memorandum and suggested cable which the Board sent to Mr. Stettinius some time before I left Washington. . . .

Pell tells me that until a short while ago he had an assistant by the name of Lawrence Preuss, who was sent to him by the Department of State and who claimed that he was in a position to speak the Department's views concerning the work of the Commission. At one time Pell prepared a memorandum for the Law Committee in which he suggested that the Commission concern itself with crimes committed by one German against another German, against a stateless person, or against a national of a German ally. Before giving such document to the Committee, he did not consult Preuss for, as Pell put it, Pruess [sic] was his subordinate sent over here to advise him, and in this case he felt that he did not need his advice. However, he took Preuss with him to the meeting at which he gave the Committee his memorandum, and to his utter surprise and amazement Preuss spoke against the memorandum and said that it did not represent the views of the Department of State. Preuss continually opposed Pell in his efforts and eventually went back to the Department of State where, presumably, he now is. However, before going he told the clerks in Pell's office that he would see to it that the War Crimes Commission did nothing for the Jews. . . .

Sincerely yours,
James H. Mann

* * *

Memorandum Re Jurisdiction of War Crimes Commission over Murder of Jews, December 23, 1944, probably authored by DuBois:[67]

Last August in London Mr. DuBois learned from Mr. Herbert Pell, American Representative on the War Crimes Commission, that most of the Commission's members were of the opinion that the term "war crime," as defined by the Commission, did not include acts committed by the Nazis and their satellites against Jews of "Axis" nationality and other stateless persons. This would mean that persons guilty of atrocities against German, Hungarian, Bulgarian and Rumanian Jews would escape punishment as war criminals unless they also happened to have committed crimes against United Nations nationals. Mr. Pell indicated that the view of the Commission might well change if a strong cable of instructions were received from Washington setting forth the disagreement of the United States Government with any such restrictive definition of the term "war crime."

2. On August 28, Mr. Pehle transmitted a memorandum to Mr. Stettinius recommending that a cable be sent to Mr. Pell advising him of the declared policy of this Government that all Axis nationals guilty of atrocities, regardless of whether the victims were or were not of the same nationality as the criminals, should be tried and punished as war criminals. On September 4, Mr. Pehle received a reply stating that the War Refugee Board would be advised as soon as a decision was reached within the Department of State.

3. Nothing further was heard from the Department of State. Each time that an inquiry was made by telephone—and there were more than five such inquiries in the past three months—the Board was advised that the matter was still "under consideration" by the Office of the Legal Adviser to the Secretary of State and the War and Navy Departments.

4. When Mr. Herbert Pell called on Mr. DuBois two weeks ago asking why he had not received a cable of instructions from Washington, inquiry was again made of the Department of State. This time the Board's representative received the "impression" that the State Department had been unable to find a "legal theory" to justify the punishment of Germans for killing German and other Axis Jews. Four or five days later, a letter was received from Mr. Stettinius stating that the whole war crimes situation was still under "active consideration" by the Department of State and other interested Departments.

5. Mr. Pehle and Mr. Friedman have since had another discussion with a representative of the Department of State with regard to the question of war crimes. They were advised confidentially that the War and State Departments are "considering" what action can be taken and propose to submit a program to the President within the near future.

* * *

Excerpts from an untitled and undated memorandum by Herbert Pell, written in July 1945:[68]

During the summer [of 1944], a committee of the War Crimes Commission, of which I was chairman, recommended to the various governments that arrangements should be immediately made to arrest all members of the Gestapo who were captured, and that an organization along the lines of the F.B.I. should be set up to comb prisoners and the population as we go into Germany. We also recommended that courts should be set up prepared for the immediate trial of war criminals. We particularly recommended the setting up of international military courts which could be expanded ad lib. It was manifest that it would take time to organize such courts and to get the machinery ready. We believed that all of this should be done before the actual occupation of Germany so that the trials could commence as soon as possible. . . . The last of these recommendations came over here in October 1944, and lay in [the files of] Mr. [Green] Hackworth [legal adviser to the State Department], so far as I know, untouched. Certainly nothing was done about it.

I returned about the 6th of December, 1944 to report and to see how things were getting on. I was shocked to find that the State Department, under Mr. Stettinius and Mr. Hackworth had done absolutely nothing about these recommendations and apparently had no intention whatsoever of moving. I protested against this and endeavored to see the President, who was then preparing for his trip to Yalta. I managed to get an interview with him on the 9th of January. Before seeing him, I went to Mr. Hackworth's office and asked him if there had been any developments of which the President should be informed. He told me, "No, there had been no change." I then went over and talked to the President who quite agreed with my contention that the Gestapo should be punished to a man; and, as Sir Cecil Hurst, the British representative and chairman of the Commission, had resigned, he told me that I should take the place myself. His last words to me were, "Go back as quickly as you can and get yourself appointed chairman." That afternoon, I went over to see Secretary Stettinius, thinking that I would just shake him by the hand and take the first ship back to England. When I arrived at his office, Mr. Hackworth was there who said that the last Congress which had adjourned on the 19th of December, about three weeks before, had failed to make any appropriations for the War Crimes Commission, and therefore, I could not go back. This rather surprised me. I pointed out to Mr. Hackworth that as he had known this in the morning before I went to see the President, he should have told me. He said, "You were the President's appointee and not mine, and it was none of my business to inform you." Mr. Stettinius upheld him on this.

It is perfectly obvious that all this was designed to get me out because I had so vigorously upheld the cause of the victims in Germany. My place was taken by Colonel [Joseph V.] Hodgson, who apparently could take the place because he was paid by the War Department and not the State Department. The State Department, however, found enough money to pay the rest of the office and all the other expenses of the Commission. All Mr. Hackworth lacked was money to pay me. I offered to serve for nothing, but he said this could not be done either.

* * *

Excerpts from a memorandum, apparently written in February 1945, probably by Samuel Merlin, a leader of the Bergson Group:[69]

... Immediately after New Year's Day, the State Department announced that Herbert C. Pell, head of the American delegation on the War Crimes Commission, was not returning to London because Congress had failed to appropriate the money for his expenses. Through friendly sources, Mr. Peter Bergson learned that the statement of the State Department was not as candid as it appeared and that the real reason for Mr. Pell's failure to return to London lay in the fact that he insisted on the approval by our Government of the decision of the War Crimes Commission to regard the crimes committed against the Hebrew people, whatever their legal citizenship, as war crimes.

Mr. Bergson went on to see Mr. Pell and discovered that this elderly gentleman, who had held some of the most important diplomatic posts in Europe, felt completely defeated by the attitude and action of the State Department. "There is nothing left for me to do," he said to Mr. Bergson "but move from Washington to the Knickerbockers Club in New York. I can see no further service that I can render to my government and to the unfortunate Hebrew people in Europe."

At the end of two hours' conversation, Mr. Bergson persuaded Mr. Pell that there was a great deal that could still be done. He convinced him that the whole case could be blasted wide open in the newspapers and Mr. Pell consented to hold a press conference for that purpose. We organized this press conference and forced the issue into the open. Mr. Pell made a remarkably forceful statement that won front-page prominence in New York and Washington papers. It put the State Department on the defensive and forced both Secretary Stettinius and Undersecretary [Joseph C.] Grew to issue statements indicating that our Government would insist on the punishment of those guilty of crimes against the Hebrew people.

* * *

Excerpt from the New York Times, *February 2, 1945 (for the complete text of this article, see Appendix 2):*

Grew Widens Area of Nazi War Crime
By Bertram D. Hulen

Washington, Feb. 1—Germans responsible for crimes within the Reich, including those against Jews and others, beyond any question will be punished, Joseph C. Grew, acting Secretary of State, announced today.

In a statement defining the American position on the question, Mr. Grew ... said: "Over the past months, officers of the Department of State, in consultation with other departments, have worked out proposals as forthright and far-reaching as the objectives announced by the President, which they are intended to implement. They provide for the punishment of German leaders and their associates for their responsibility for the whole broad criminal enterprise devised and executed with ruthless disregard of the very foundations of law and morality, including offenses wherever committed against the rules of war and against minority elements, Jewish and other groups, and individuals." . . .

* * *

VIII. Summing Up

Q:[70] Looking back on it, how would you sum up the deeds that were accomplished [by the War Refugee Board]?

McCLELLAND: The accomplishments in mathematical terms were pretty small. But I still feel that it was worth doing. We certainly didn't redeem ourselves entirely, but we did it to a small extent—we, the United States—by undertaking this eleventh hour effort. One simply regrets bitterly that we did not mobilize ourselves earlier on and devote more resources.

* * *

Q:[71] Do you feel more could have been done to save Jews if a bigger effort had been made earlier?

HIRSCHMANN: It was very obvious, as one who was there, that it was possible to rescue people by informal methods, by bribery, chicanery, or resourceful contacting which I attempted to effectuate with the power that I had with the backing of the United States. We must remember that at that time, the United States was the great power in the world, and while we were some thousands of miles away, the use of power, not only the implied used of it, could have been used had we done something with it. In my final report to the State Department, I said—and if I may, I'll just quote these few words—"It bears repetition that it is regrettable that the Board, which has demonstrated the success and the vitality of its operations was not created a year or two ago. There is no doubt from the evidence at hand that additional thousands of refugees could have been saved, the mere existence of the Board and its representatives in Turkey acted as a catalytic agent, spurring the morale of the destitute, terrorized citizens of the Balkans and provided for the victims a ray of hope." And in conclusion, I must repeat what [Alexander] Cretzianu [the Rumanian ambassador in Ankara] said to me, "If it meant so much to your government to save these people, why didn't you come earlier?"

* * *

EDWARD BERNSTEIN:[72] Josiah DuBois had a great sense of the obligation of the government to do justice and to help those oppressed. And he was always concerned, far more than anyone else, about the importance of the government of the United States to save the Jews of Europe.

Q: What drove him?

BERNSTEIN: Why should we think that a person needs extra motivation because he is not a Jew? These are problems that transcend sectarian faith.

* * *

Q:[73] Why did people like you and Pehle do it?

DuBois: Well, we felt very strongly that this was a terrible thing that was happening and we felt it our duty to do what we could.

Notes

1. For the full text of Executive Order 9417, see Appendix 1.

2. Martin Ostrow interview with John Pehle, Bethesda, Maryland, 2 October 1991.

3. Laurence Jarvik interview with John Pehle, Washington, D.C., 16 October 1978, transcript in the possession of the author.

4. Laurence Jarvik interview with Josiah E. DuBois, Jr., Camden, NJ, 23 October 1978.

5. Jarvik interview with DuBois, op. cit.

6. Baruch Korff (1914–1995), an activist rabbi from Boston, was involved with both the Emergency Committee to Save the Jewish People of Europe and the Vaad Ha-hatzala. In 1945, he established the Political Action Committee for Palestine, a Bergson-style group that used newspaper ads, rallies, and theatrical events to publicize the plight of Holocaust survivors and promote the cause of creating a Jewish state. In 1947, he was imprisoned for some weeks in France on charges of conspiring to drop Zionist leaflets from an airplane over London. After the establishment of Israel in 1948, he returned to the pulpit, serving as spiritual leader of congregations in New Hampshire and Massachusetts and as chaplain for two Massachusetts hospitals. In later years, he attracted attention as founder of the National Citizens' Committee for Fairness to the President, which publicly defended President Richard M. Nixon during the Watergate crisis.

7. Baruch Korff, *Flight from Fear* (New York: Elmar, 1953), 43.

8. John W. McCormack (1891–1980), Democrat of Massachusetts, was first elected to the United States House of Representatives in 1928, and served continuously until 1971.

9. Morgenthau interview with Klotz, op. cit.

10. Rabbi Abraham Kalmanowitz (1891–1965) was the dean of the Mirrer Yeshiva, a renowned Orthodox rabbinical academy in Poland. He immigrated to the United States in 1940 and soon became one of the leaders of the Vaad ha-Hatzala, the refugee rescue committee established by the Union of Orthodox Rabbis of the United States.

11. MD 4/6/44, 87.

12. War Refugee Board staff member Florence Hodel.

13. Morgenthau interview with Klotz, op. cit.

14. Rafael Medoff telephone interview with Rabbi Levi Horowitz, the Bostoner Rebbe, 1 January 2006.

15. Korff, 44–45.

16. MD 718/172–173.

17. James M. Mead (1885–1964), Democrat of New York, was first elected to the United States House of Representatives in 1919 and served until 1938, when he was chosen to fill a vacancy left by the death of U.S. Senator Royal S. Copeland. Mead served in the Senate until 1947.

18. Jarvik interview with DuBois, op. cit.

19. Korff, 45.

20. Jarvik interview with DuBois, op. cit.

21. From remarks made by Mr. Goodwin at "Blowing the Whistle on Genocide: Josiah E. DuBois, Jr., and the Struggle for a U.S. Response to the Holocaust," The University of Pennsylvania School of Law, 11 June 2006.

22. MD 719/158.

23. A.E. Clattenburg, State Department, "Memorandum of Conference," 10 April 1944, NA, SD 840.48 Refugees/3-2344.

24. Korff, 45–48.

25. Jarvik interview with DuBois, op. cit.; Morgenthau interview with DuBois, op. cit..

26. The accounts provided by Josiah DuBois in postwar interviews (cited above) state that he was the one who leaked the story to Pearson. DuBois makes no mention of Rabbi Korff's contacting Pearson. Yet Korff's autobiography states that he, Korff, was the one who leaked the story, and he makes no mention of DuBois as the leaker. Both accounts are at least partly corroborated by other documents. It may be that both Du-Bois and Korff contacted Pearson separately. Alternatively, it is possible that DuBois and Korff privately agreed that DuBois would leak the story and Korff would accept responsibility for the leak in order to protect DuBois.

27. Segal to Slawson, 20 April 1944, Box 14—File: U.S. Gov't: War Refugee Board 1944, American Jewish Committee Papers, YIVO Institute, New York City.

28. Jacob Landau (1892–1952), founder and director of the Jewish Telegraphic Agency, cooperated closely with the American Jewish Committee.

29. Morgenthau interview with Pehle, op. cit.

30. Ostrow interview with Pehle, op. cit.

31. The response of Pope Pius XII and the Vatican to the persecution of Europe's Jews has been the subject of considerable controversy. Scholars such as Michael Phayer (*The Catholic Church and the Holocaust* [Bloomington: Indiana University Press, 2000]), Susan Zuccotti (*Under His Very Windows: The Vatican and the Holocaust in Italy* [New Haven: Yale University Press, 2000]), and Daniel Goldhagen (*A Moral Reckoning: The Role of the Catholic Church in the Holocaust and Its Unfulfilled Duty of Repair* [New York: Alfred A. Knopf, 2003]) emphasize that Pius failed to include the Jews by name in his few public statements criticizing Nazi brutality; the Vatican declined to give the Allies information it received about the mass killings; and the Pope said nothing before, during, or after the Nazi roundup of 1,200 Jews in Rome in October 1943 even though they were held for two days at a site right in front of the Vatican before being deported to Auschwitz.

    Pius's defenders, such as David Dalin (*The Myth of Hitler's Pope* [Chicago: Regnery, 2005]) contend that any Papal denunciations of the Holocaust might have provoked the Germans to retaliate against the Pope, the Vatican, or the city of Rome. They also stress that thousands of Jewish children were hidden in convents or with Catholic families, although critics respond, first, that such action was taken by individuals without the Vatican's support and, second, that recently discovered documents indicate the Vatican ordered that the children not be returned to Jewish auspices. Elaine Sciolino and Jason Horowitz, "Saving Jewish Children, but at What Cost?" *New York Times*, 9 January 2005, 6.

32. MD, 714/217–218.

33. M.J. Nurenberger interview with Hillel Kook, Kfar Shmaryahu, Israel, 1 July 1971.

34. Ira Hirschmann (1901–1989), a business executive, held senior positions with Lord & Taylor, Saks Fifth Avenue, and Bloomingdale's. He was also a close associate of New York City Mayor Fiorello La Guardia.

35. Johan J. Smertenko (1897–1983), born in Russia but raised in the United States, was a professor of English at Barnard, Skidmore, and Hunter Colleges. He was active in the Revisionist Zionist movement and the Bergson Group.

36. When Jarvik asked Hirschmann about his personal motivation for taking part in the rescue work, he replied: "I had been restless about the subject as soon as I heard what was happening, but I, by accident I ran into Hitler on a trip to Berlin in 1932, principally to take a music lesson from [classical pianist] Arthur Schnabel (1882–1951). I ran into a political meeting in a small hall in Berlin where I saw a man ranting at a small distance who looked somewhat like Charlie Chaplin, and it turned out to be Adolf Hitler, and what he said charged me at the moment—he didn't say it, he screamed in this hysterical voice which I can almost hear in my memory—"When I become chancellor of Germany and Austria, I will kill all the Jews. Not only here, but all over the world." I think that was the first time I really realized I was a Jew. I had paid little attention to that subject, being involved in public affairs and merchandising music, and I walked the streets of Berlin that night and made up my mind that something had to be done to expose what Hitler had said. Now he was not chancellor yet, but the screaming of his audience was so convincing to me, that they supported him, that I could see at once that he was going to become the chancellor."

37. Laurence Jarvik interview with Ira Hirschmann, New York, NY, 20 January 1979.

38. John Pehle, Memorandum for the Files, 8 March 1944, MD 707, 242–243.

39. Pehle to Morgenthau, 3 November 1944, MD 791, 103–104.

40. File: War Refugee Board, Vol. 1, Box 27, War Refugee Board Papers, Franklin D. Roosevelt Presidential Library, Hyde Park, NY.

41. State Department Record 210, War Relocation Authority, Emergency Shelter, Temporary Havens in the U.S., folder 2, National Archives.

42. Jarvik interview with DuBois, op. cit.

43. For three days, they hid in a hollowed-out woodpile near the edge of the camp. On the advice of Soviet prisoners of war, the fugitives sprinkled the area with tobacco and gasoline, which confused the German dogs that were used to search for them. On their second day in the woodpile, Vrba and Wetzler heard Allied warplanes overhead. "They came closer and closer—then bombs began to crunch not far away," Vrba later recalled. "Our pulses quickened. Were they going to bomb the camp? Was the secret out? . . . Was this the end of Auschwitz?" Actually, the Allied planes were bombing German oil factories in and around the Auschwitz complex. The idea of bombing the death camp had not yet been raised, and details such as the location of the gas chambers and crematoria were not yet known—but that was about to change.

44. The Auschwitz report received substantial coverage in the American press. It was one of the rare occasions on which a Holocaust-related article appeared on the front page of the *New York Times*, according to Prof. Laurel Leff, *Buried by the* Times*: The Holocaust and America's Most Important Newspaper* (New York: Cambridge University Press, 2005), 290. However, Leff notes, the front-page portion of the *Times* article emphasized that "Jews and Christians alike" were being murdered by the Nazis, and only in the continuation of the article, inside the paper, was it made clear that the vast majority of the Auschwitz victims were Jews. Moreover, she writes, "the *Times* never

ran an editorial [about the Vrba Wetzler report], nor did it mention [it] in the Week in Review section."

Vrba's memoir of his experiences in the Holocaust, *I Cannot Forgive* (New York: Grove Press) was published in 1964. After the war, Vrba settled in Vancouver, BC, where he remained until he passed away in 2005.

45. Ostrow interview with Pehle, op. cit.

46. File: German Extermination Camps, Box 6, War Refugee Board Papers, FDRL.

47. Francis Cardinal Spellman (1889–1967) served as the Archbishop of New York from April 1939 until his death.

48. Ibid.

49. Cited in David S. Wyman, *The Abandonment of the Jews: America and the Holocaust, 1941–1945* (New York: Pantheon, 1984), 337.

50. Jarvik interview with DuBois, op. cit.

51. MD, 716/171–175.

52. MD, 726/33–39.

53. Laurence Jarvik interview with Roswell McClelland, 16 August 1980, New York, NY. McClleland (1914–1995) served as director of the American Friends [Quakers] Service Committee's refugee relief programs in Switzerland before he was appointed as the War Refugee Board's representative there. In later years, he served as U.S. ambassador to Niger.

54. An international Orthodox Jewish organization. Isaac and Reicha Sternbuch were its chief representatives in Switzerland and spearheaded numerous efforts to rescue Jews from the Holocaust.

55. File: Hungary No. 5, Box 35, War Refugee Board Papers, FDRL.

56. Wyman 1984, 99.

57. Ostrow interview with Pehle, op. cit.

58. Haim Hecht and Stuart Erdheim interview with George S. McGovern, 28 December 2004, South Dakota, Archives of the David S. Wyman Institute for Holocaust Studies.

59. Elie Wiesel, *Night* (New York: Avon, 1969), 71.

60. File: Hungary No. 5, Box 35, War Refugee Board Papers, FDRL. Latvian-born Benjamin Akzin (1904–1985), a political scientist, was a senior official of the Revisionist Zionist movement in Europe during the 1920s and 1930s. After moving to the United States in 1940, he served as head of the Legal Department of the Library of Congress from 1941 to 1944 before joining the staff of the War Refugee Board. After the war, he became a senior adviser to Rabbi Dr. Abba Hillel Silver, head of the American Zionist Emergency Council. Settling in Israel in 1949, Akzin became a law professor at Hebrew University, and later served as rector and acting president of the University of Haifa.

61. Rafael Medoff interview with Richard C. Goodwin, Newark, NJ, 23 May 2005.

62. NA, MB Record Group 107, Assistant Secretary of War Files, 400.38 Countries C-D-E-F (Box 151).

63. NA, MB Record Group 107, Assistant Secretary of War Files, 400.38 Countries—Germany.

64. MD, 805/8–9, 11–14, 16–17.

65. Ibid.

66. Mann to Pehle, 19 September 1944, File: England (James Mann), Box 70, WRB, FDRL.

67. MD, 805/8–9, 11–14, 16–17.

68. Personal files of Senator Claiborne Pell, courtesy of David S. Wyman.

69. File: Hebrew Committee of National Liberation—February 1945, Box 1, Folder 16, PSGP.

70. Jarvik interview with McClelland, op. cit.

71. Jarvik interview with Hirschmann, op. cit.

72. Martin Ostrow interview with Edward Bernstein, Washington, D.C., 7 February 1992.

73. Jarvik interview with DuBois, op. cit.

CHAPTER SIX

The War Refugee Board: A Summary of Its Achievements[1]

Executive Order 9417 establishing the War Refugee Board endowed it with great potential. It directed the State, Treasury, and War Departments to provide whatever help the board needed to implement its rescue programs, subject only to the stipulation that they be "consistent with the successful prosecution of the war." In addition, it required all other government agencies to comply with the board's requests for assistance.

This order, which carried the force of law, should have opened the way for a powerful rescue campaign. But the WRB did not receive the cooperation that was promised. As a result, its capacity for rescue was always substantially less than it should have been. Only the Treasury Department met its full responsibilities. Besides housing the WRB and providing most of its staff, Secretary Morgenthau himself kept in close touch with the board.

Secretary of War Stimson believed in the WRB's mission but could spare almost no time for it because of his many other duties. The job of War Department liaison with the board fell to Assistant Secretary John J. McCloy. Although on the surface he seemed concerned about the plight of Europe's Jews, McCloy was privately skeptical that the military should take a role in their rescue. The War Department's contribution to the work of the board was very small.

Cordell Hull, who preferred that the State Department's connection with the WRB be limited, designated Undersecretary Edward R. Stettinius, Jr., as his representative. Stettinius had welcomed the board's formation, but he, too, made little time for rescue matters. As a result, George Warren of the President's Advisory Committee on Political Refugees served as State's primary liaison with the WRB. Despite his long service in the area of refugee aid, Warren did little to counteract the opposition to the board that prevailed among the department's middle-level officials.

The WRB staff, which never numbered more than thirty, revolved around a dozen people, most of them non-Jewish and most of them veterans of Treasury's battles with State over the rescue issue. They were, as one observer remarked, "young, dynamic, bold, clear and a bit brash."[2] John Pehle was executive director. Josiah E. DuBois, Jr., was general counsel and author of many of its project proposals.

During February and March 1944, the WRB chose representatives to direct its overseas operations and assigned them to locations that bordered Axis Europe: Turkey, Switzerland, Sweden, North Africa, Italy, and Portugal. They were granted diplomatic status as special attachés to the American missions there. But the WRB's efforts to place representatives in Russia, Spain, and Egypt failed. The Soviet government was unresponsive. The American ambassador to Spain, Carlton J.H. Hayes, opposed the move. And the State Department blocked the board's attempt to send Charles R. Joy to Egypt; Joy (and his employer, the Unitarian Service Committee) had been too outspoken and too politically active to satisfy State's standards.

From the start, the WRB solicited advice from many private agencies involved in rescue and relief activities. Nearly a score of them submitted comprehensive suggestions. Once in action, the board regularly coordinated its projects with those of the private groups and arranged to use the State Department's coded telegraphic communications system for transmission of messages between the American private agencies and their representatives overseas.

Under pressure from Stettinius, the State Department sent to all American diplomatic missions abroad cablegrams drafted by the board and ordering full cooperation with it. Special instructions were dispatched to those in neutral nations close to Nazi territory directing them to urge the governments to permit entry of all refugees who reached their borders and to publicize their willingness to take them in. The board assured the neutral powers that it would provide maintenance for the newly arrived refugees and arrange their evacuation as soon as possible. The WRB also offered its assistance to the International Red Cross.

But middle-level State officials, who had been thrust aside in the first rush of WRB action, soon moved to reestablish their grip on diplomatic affairs. By mid-March, six urgent WRB cablegrams were stuck in the State Department awaiting clearance. Delays hobbled such important measures as warnings to Axis satellites to refrain from collaborating in atrocities and efforts to persuade the British to set up a refugee camp in Libya. The problem eased somewhat by April. But instead of providing the nearly unlimited help that had been promised in Executive Order 9417, the State Department often stood in the way of board operations. The same was true, although less frequently, of the War Department.

Another impediment was the British refusal to establish a parallel rescue committee to work with the WRB. Only grudgingly did British officials cooperate with the board's efforts to evacuate refugees from the Balkans through Turkey to Palestine. They attempted to restrict the activities of the WRB representative in southern Italy. And they persistently tried to block the board's program of licensing private agencies to transmit relief money to Europe.

Probably the most crucial difficulty to confront the WRB concerned funds. From the beginning, the board acted mainly as facilitator and coordinator of projects carried out by the private organizations. Even when it initiated rescue operations, it usually called on the private agencies to fund them. Although rescue had finally become official government policy, American Jews through contributions to their own organizations had to pay most of the costs.

In its sixteen months of action, the WRB spent $547,000 of government funds, drawn from $1,150,000 set aside for it in the President's Emergency Fund. The $547,000 went largely for salaries and other administrative expenses. In addition, the president allotted the board $1,068,750 to buy and ship food parcels to concentration camp inmates. The other projects sponsored by the WRB were funded almost entirely by the Jewish organizations. The Joint Distribution Committee spent in excess of $15,000,000; the Vaad ha-Hatzala (Orthodox rescue committee) supplied over $1,000,000; the World Jewish Congress expended more than $300,000; and other groups provided lesser amounts.

What looked at first as if it might become a potent government rescue machine turned into a valuable but limited collaboration between the government and private agencies. Nevertheless, the WRB staff was determined to do all it could. Working mainly with proposals that Jewish organizations had long been urging, the WRB forged a wide-ranging rescue program, including (1) evacuating Jews and other endangered people from Axis territory, (2) finding places to which they could be sent, (3) using psychological measures (especially threats of war-crimes trials) aimed at preventing deportations and atrocities, and (4) shipping relief supplies into concentration camps.

As for evacuation, the potential outlets were Turkey, Spain, Allied-occupied southern Italy, Sweden, and Switzerland.

Turkey

The first WRB representative to see action overseas was Ira Hirschmann, a prominent New York department-store executive who had attended the ill-fated Evian Conference of 1938 and afterwards continued to be deeply concerned about the European Jews. His post, Turkey, offered important possibilities for rescue because hundreds of thousands of Jews were still alive—and in danger—in the nearby Balkans.

Hirschmann persuaded the Turkish government to allow 200 Jews to enter from Bulgaria and continue on to Palestine every ten days. Only 131 came during the first month of the arrangement, and the numbers subsequently decreased. Much of the problem stemmed from a tight Bulgarian policy on the exit of Jews, but Turkey also kept the influx down by insisting on advance procurement of Turkish transit visas while quietly making them practically unavailable.

By the end of the summer of 1944, the WRB had brought only about 450 Jews out of Bulgaria.

In late March, the Jewish Agency (Palestine Jewry's governing body), with the WRB's support and Joint Distribution Committee funds, initiated a limited exodus from Rumania to Turkey by hiring three Bulgarian boats (at exorbitant rates). These tiny vessels, unseaworthy and overloaded, running belligerent waters without safe-conduct assurances, brought out 1,200 people. During July and early August, they moved 1,500 refugees from Rumania to Turkey.

Another escape route, across the Aegean Sea from Greece to Turkey, saved about 900 Jews during the year prior to Greece's liberation in October 1944.

As noted in chapter five, Hirschmann's most impressive achievement involved Rumania, not Turkey. The German army, falling back before the Soviets, was entering Transnistria, an area of Rumania where many thousands of Jews were living in terrible camps. The Jews were situated in the path of the retreat. As a result of Hirschmann's intervention, the Rumanian government agreed to transfer the Jews from Transnistria to the interior of Rumania. Thus the 48,000 Jews still alive in Transnistria were safeguarded.

In all, nearly 7,000 Jews left the Balkans and reached Palestine via Turkey under the aegis of the WRB. Far larger numbers were saved by breaking up the abominable Transnistrian camps and bargaining for the greatest possible protection for Jews who were still alive in Rumania and Bulgaria. Hirschmann pointed out that the very formation of the WRB had accomplished something else of importance. Its birth, according to numerous Jews passing through Turkey, had "injected new life and hope into . . . refugees throughout the European continent." One group of fugitives explained, with obvious emotion, "For two years there has been only one phrase on everyone's lips, 'When are the Americans coming?'"

Spain

After Turkey, Spain appeared to be the most important escape hatch from Axis Europe. The basic WRB plan for Spain called for the American ambassador, Carlton J.H. Hayes, to urge the Spanish government to relax its border restrictions and publicly announce its willingness to receive refugees. Spain should also be asked to set up three reception camps along the French border. They would remain under Spanish control, but the WRB would finance them, moving refugees through them promptly, and then out of Spain.

The board succeeded in mid-February 1944 in persuading the State Department to instruct Hayes to press the WRB rescue plan with the Spanish government. But Hayes replied that he did not believe the plan would increase the refugee flow and that he would not present it. He asserted that relaxation of Spain's border controls would only facilitate entry of German agents and encourage efforts to smuggle wolfram (tungsten) out of Spain to German purchasers. Germany depended on Spain and Portugal for its supply of wolfram, and Hayes was negotiating with Spain for full stoppage of wolfram exports to Germany. Hayes also tried to keep rescue funds from going into Spain.

No amount of pressure could change Hayes's position. He also kept the board from placing its representative in Spain. The stalemate continued until Hayes visited the United States in mid-July 1944. He then reluctantly agreed to accept the WRB's James H. Mann as representative—for a two-month trial period. A month later, the State Department approved Mann. But by then the Allies were far along in the reconquest of France. The chance for important rescue work through Spain had passed.

The WRB had visualized Spain as a conveyor belt, moving many refugees to freedom. That hope was dashed utterly. In contrast, the WRB encountered no difficulties in the other Iberian nation, Portugal. The American minister there, R. Henry Norwed, cooperated fully. On the WRB's assurance that the United States would move them to other places, the Portuguese government agreed to open its doors to all refugees coming through Spain. But very few arrived, for that conduit never opened.

Southern Italy

Allied advances in Italy following the invasion of September 1943 opened another escape route from Axis Europe. By November, refugees were streaming across the Adriatic Sea from Yugoslavia to southern Italy in an exodus largely organized by the Tito-led Yugoslav resistance movement.

Until March 1944, the Allied military cooperated fully with this Yugoslav evacuation. The British navy transported thousands of refugees across the Adriatic. Thousands more came in small partisan boats. The British army sheltered and fed the fugitives in Italy and, using two troop ships, transferred them to camps in El Shatt and Khatatba, in Egypt. Nearly all of these refugees were Yugoslav civilians. Few were Jewish. (The Nazis had already murdered most Yugoslav Jews.) The Jews among them (about 500 of the first 15,000) remained in Italy because the British camp administration in Egypt opposed bringing Jews there.

By spring 1944, El Shatt and Khatatba were three-fourths full, and refugees were still entering Italy at the rate of 1,800 per week. Concerned that the camps in Egypt would reach capacity and the escapees then pile up in Italy, the military authorities issued orders to discourage further refugee movement across the Adriatic, cutting the influx by two-thirds.

In March, Leonard E. Ackerman, the WRB's representative in North Africa, was appointed its representative in Italy as well. He learned of the military's order to slow the refugee flow into Italy. Ackerman and the board in Washington recognized that a crisis had arisen. If the Adriatic route closed, the chance of opening an outlet from Hungary would also disappear. At that time, May 1944, Adolph Eichmann and his henchmen were concentrating massive numbers of Hungarian Jews for deportation. The long, crowded death trains had already started to wind through the Slovakian mountains to Auschwitz.

In Washington, Morgenthau called the situation to President Roosevelt's attention at a cabinet meeting, and the president responded that the refugee flow across the Adriatic must not be hindered. Instructions went at once to the military in Italy to lift the restriction. The president agreed to a WRB proposal to move one thousand refugees from Italy to an emergency internment camp in the United States and ordered an intensive search for havens in the Mediterranean area.

Allied military authorities quickly found that they could accommodate many more refugees in Italy. They also initiated steps to open a camp at Philippeville in French North Africa, for up to 7,000 people. And the United Nations Relief and Rehabilitation Administration, which had recently taken over the Egyptian camps, increased their capacity from 30,000 to 40,000. The Adriatic route was used all summer, but by late August, the Nazi threat to Yugoslav civilians had virtually ended. When the exodus stopped in September 1944 over 36,000 Yugoslavs, nearly all non-Jews, had escaped to Italy. About 28,000 had moved on to the camps in Egypt; the rest remained in Italy until they were repatriated.

Sweden

In Sweden, determined work by the WRB representative, Iver C. Olsen, brought limited results. Olsen organized and funded committees that sent rescue teams across the Baltic Sea into Estonia, Latvia, and Lithuania to bring out Jews and non-Jewish political refugees. These units obtained fast cabin cruisers, fuel, supplies, and false identification papers. But although the program operated throughout the summer of 1944, it rescued only 1,200 people, none of them Jews. Most Jews still alive in the Baltic states were in hiding. Many could have fled on WRB boats, but they suspected a German trap and would not take the risk.

But the WRB's Swedish effort did accomplish a little for Jewish refugees. With the assistance of the American minister in Sweden, Herschel V. Johnson, Olsen persuaded the Swedish government to bring in the 150 Jewish refugees in Finland.

Near the end of the war, Olsen and Johnson also lent their support to a series of secret negotiations that led in April 1945 to the transfer of two groups of concentration camp inmates to Sweden. The first to come out were 425 Jews whom the Nazis had deported from Denmark. Soon afterward, 7,000 women, half of them Jews, arrived in Sweden from the wretched Ravensbruck camp.

Switzerland

The WRB accomplished more in Switzerland than in Spain, Italy, or Sweden. Because of its location close to much of Nazi Europe, it became the board's overseas nerve center. It was the best corridor for sending funds into Europe and a vital relay point for communications in and out of Axis territory.

The WRB was fortunate to find a highly qualified person already in Switzerland to serve as its representative. Roswell McClelland, director of the American Friends Service Committee's refugee-relief program there, enjoyed good relations with other such groups, many with underground connections and communications networks reaching into Nazi Europe.

From a discretionary fund of $250,000 supplied by the Joint Distribution Committee, McClelland financed numerous undercover programs: relief operations in Axis territory, production of false documents, an underground courier service, and escape projects. Conducted for the most part by already existing underground and resistance groups, board operations extended into France, Germany, Italy, Czechoslovakia, and Hungary. They enabled thousands of endangered people in Axis Europe to survive and thousands more to escape.

The WRB sent funds from Switzerland to contribute to maintenance of the nearly 8,000 Jewish orphans hidden in France in Christian homes, schools, and convents. It was anxious to move the most endangered of the children to Switzerland, but the Swiss government would not accept them unless a responsible government guaranteed to remove them when the war ended. The British refused, insisting that they could not reserve Palestine certificates for after the war. The State Department, under WRB pressure, authorized postwar immigration of up to 4,000 of the children, and the program went forward. By August 1944, when the threat had passed in France, 650 of the orphans had reached Switzerland and about 600 other Jewish children had entered with their parents or relatives.

Hungary

During its sixteen months of active service, the War Refugee Board encountered an endless procession of difficult problems. But it never confronted any greater challenge than the Nazi campaign to annihilate the 760,000 Jews in Hungary. The Hungarian crisis began when the board was only eight weeks old. It lasted nearly a year.

Until 1944, despite severe anti-Semitic restrictions, Hungary had permitted its large Jewish population to live in a semblance of peace. It had even served as a refuge for several thousand Jews from Poland and Slovakia. But on March 19, 1944, fearing that Hungary would defect to the Allies and angry at its failure to deport the Jews into Nazi hands, Hitler sent occupying forces into the nation. The arch-organizer of deportation, Adolf Eichmann, arrived in Budapest soon afterward and, drawing on extensive Hungarian collaboration, set his operation in motion. In mid-April, the concentration of Jews into central locations began. On May 15, mass deportations to Auschwitz commenced.

Because of the extreme difficulty of organizing direct rescue from Hungary, surrounded as it was by Axis territory, the WRB had to rely heavily on psychological approaches. In April, when it first learned of the impending danger, the board sent stern warnings to Hungary through neutral channels. Directly after the deportations started, it urged the neutral countries, the Vatican, and the International Red Cross (IRC) to assign additional diplomatic personnel to Hungary as a restraining influence. Sweden and the Vatican soon complied; the IRC did eventually. Spain, Portugal, Switzerland, and Turkey did not. The WRB also appealed to the neutrals to grant protective citizenship documents to Hungarian Jews who had family or business ties to their countries. The cooperation of all but Turkey ultimately contributed to the safekeeping of thousands of Jews.

President Roosevelt publicly condemned the Nazi atrocities and promised that "none who participate in these acts of savagery shall go unpunished." The Office of War Information and the BBC broadcast warning messages of retaliation to Hungary and other parts of Europe. The OWI had the warnings publicized throughout the neutral European press and radio. And Allied aircraft dropped them into Hungary in pamphlet form.

Meanwhile, the WRB pressed the neutral nations, the International Red Cross, and the Vatican to urge the Hungarian government to stop the deportations. On June 25, Pope Pius XII telegraphed a personal appeal to the Hungarian head of state, Regent Miklos Horthy. The king of Sweden, Gustav V, also sent a personal plea to Horthy, asking him "in the name of humanity" to save the remaining Jews. IRC president Max Huber dispatched a handwritten letter to Horthy that summarized recent shocking reports about Auschwitz and requested detailed information on what was happening to the deported Jews. But by July 6, the day Huber's message was sent, the earlier pressures, along with Germany's declining military situation, had already induced Horthy to stand up to the Nazis at last and insist that the deportations halt. By then, almost 440,000 Jews were gone, but most of Budapest's 230,000 Jews were still in the capital. The appeals from the Pope and the king of Sweden, stimulated in part by the WRB, had been especially important in stopping the deportations.

On July 18, in a startling reply to the International Red Cross, Horthy offered to permit emigration of all Jewish children under the age of ten who possessed visas to other countries and all Jews of any age who had Palestine certificates. He also invited the Red Cross to provide relief to the Jews in Hungary. But no Jews ever left Hungary under the Horthy proposal. The Nazis, who controlled Hungary's borders, barred the doors.

Even though the emigration proposal collapsed, Horthy had opened the possibility of survival for the more than 200,000 Jews in Budapest. The deportations had stopped. The Red Cross accepted the invitation to bring in relief supplies. And neutral diplomats and the papal nuncio devised ways to safeguard tens of thousands of Jews. Palestine visas offered some protection. Thousands of them came in through Catholic diplomatic couriers and the nunciature. Baptismal certificates were issued. The Swedish, Swiss, Spanish, and Portuguese legations provided thousands of protective documents and visas. Zionist youth groups forged additional papers. The neutral legations, the church, and the Red

Cross also protected thousands of Jews by keeping them in buildings under their extraterritorial jurisdiction.

The Swedish legation led in this unusual venture in mass preservation of Jewish lives. At the center of the effort was Raoul Wallenberg, one of the main heroes in the entire struggle to counter the Holocaust. The thirty-one-year-old architect and businessman, member of a leading Swedish diplomatic and banking family, met with the WRB's Iver Olsen in Stockholm in June 1944. He offered to go to Hungary to help the Jews. At Olsen's suggestion, the Swedish government appointed him an attaché to its Budapest legation. In practice, Wallenberg served as the WRB's representative in Hungary, receiving from it suggestions for action and the funds for his mission.

Working with a staff of more than 300 people, largely volunteers, Wallenberg threw most of his efforts into plans to bring Hungarian Jews under Swedish protection. He rented a building, applied Swedish extraterritorial status to it, and used it as a safe haven for several hundred Jewish religious leaders. He also persuaded the Swedish government to allow the legation to issue special protective passports to Hungarian Jews. With time, he expanded both schemes and ultimately saved tens of thousands of Jews.

When the Russians finally captured the city in mid-February 1945, about 120,000 Jews remained alive, a significant accomplishment under the circumstances. The forces from the outside world that had pressured Horthy and the later protective measures inside Budapest were crucial in saving them. The WRB had been a decisive factor in both efforts.

How much of this was due to Raoul Wallenberg's work? He was directly responsible for rescuing at least 20,000 Jews. Similar measures by the Swiss, Spanish, and Portuguese legations, the nuncio, and the Red Cross helped save an estimated 11,000 to 30,000. Wallenberg was indirectly responsible for much of that, too, because his example had influenced the others to expand. Another 70,000 Jews who survived were huddled in the Budapest ghetto. For them, Wallenberg provided what food he could and forestalled several Arrow Cross attacks on the ghetto. Finally, as the city was about to fall, plans were under way for the last-minute destruction of the ghetto and its inhabitants. Wallenberg's threat of sure postwar punishment in a confrontation with the SS commander of Budapest may have been the decisive factor in stopping that scheme.

In May 1944, Adolf Eichmann offered, through Hungarian Zionist activist Joel Brand, to release one million Jews in return for 10,000 trucks to be used only on the eastern front, and sizable amounts of coffee, tea, cocoa, and soap. He also spoke of an indefinite amount of foreign currency. Brand traveled to Istanbul and then Aleppo, where he was arrested by the British. He relayed Eichmann's offer to the British; Jewish Agency leaders; and Ira Hirschmann, the WRB representative in Turkey. In Washington, Morgenthau and Pehle, with the concurrence of President Roosevelt, strongly supported continuing negotiations in the hope that Eichmann's offer might be the forerunner of other proposals. But British and Soviet opposition precluded pursuing it.

The Brand affair produced two concrete results. Not long after Brand left Hungary, Dr. Rudolf Kastner, a leading Hungarian Zionist, informed Eichmann that a report from Turkey indicated Allied acceptance in principle of his offer. Now, said Kastner, the Nazis should prove their seriousness. At the end of June, Eichmann permitted a special transport of almost 1,700 Jews to leave Hungary. Supposedly bound for Spain and freedom, the train instead delivered its passengers to Bergen-Belsen. The second transaction involved some 18,000 Hungarian Jews scheduled for deportation to Auschwitz. They were diverted to labor projects near Strasshof, Austria. About three-fourths of them survived the war.

In August, the WRB decided to pursue the Brand matter indirectly through Saly Mayer, the Joint Distribution Committee's representative in Switzerland. Communicating through McClelland, the WRB emphasized that no ransom arrangements were permissible and he must act only as a Swiss Jewish leader—the objective being "to draw out the negotiations and gain as much time as possible." Meanwhile, it was hoped, the remaining Jews would be permitted to live, and Allied military advances would put an end to the extermination process.

Before he would negotiate, Mayer insisted on delivery to Switzerland of an initial installment of 500 of the 1,700 Hungarian Jews who had been sent to Bergen-Belsen. Their discussions commenced on August 21 at St. Margarethen on the Swiss–Austrian border, with Kurt Becher, a high SS officer who represented Himmler. That very day, 318 Jews arrived from Bergen-Belsen.

In a series of follow-up meetings extending over six months, Mayer ingeniously stretched out the negotiations, helped by the worsening German military situation. Among his offers was that in exchange for an end to the exterminations, food would be sent into German-held territory for the IRC to distribute to the surviving Jews. The Nazi negotiators were willing to discuss the plan. McClelland backed it and endorsed Mayer's plea to the WRB to send $5 million to strengthen his bargaining position. The money arrived three weeks later in early January. But the project did not materialize.

What did Saly Mayer achieve? In August 1944, he succeeded in bringing out 318 of the Hungarian Jews who were being held in Bergen-Belsen. In early December, 1,368 other people in the original transport from Hungary also reached Switzerland. Apparently, Mayer's repeated insistence that their continued internment was impeding the discussions helped persuade the Germans to let them go.

The Search for Havens

From its inception, the War Refugee Board realized that a major obstacle to rescue was the lack of places to which Jewish refugees could go. So the board began immediately to search the world for havens. It also assisted in the final push for the long-delayed North Africa refugee camp that the Allies' Bermuda Conference in 1943 had recommended in order to clear Spain of refugees. A former American army barracks at Fedala, near Casablanca, was finally chosen, but it took almost three months to gain the consent of the authorities there, the French Committee of National Liberation. At that, the French set a limit of 2,000, although the facility could hold 15,000.

In mid-1944, the Allied Mediterranean military command, seeking to relieve the refugee buildup in southern Italy, put pressure on the French to agree to a second camp. French permission came promptly this time: a former Allied military barracks at Philippeville on the Mediterranean coast in Algeria, which could accommodate from 2,500 to 7,000. The WRB's third and last sanctuary, a camp for 1,000 refugees at Fort Ontario, New York, came only after months of effort.

At the initiative of DuBois (see chapter five), the board suggested emergency camps in the United States where refugees could be interned like prisoners of war and repatriated after Germany's defeat. The whole operation would take place outside the immigration system, avoiding any question of altering quotas or visa procedures. The WRB drafted a memorandum for the president emphasizing that no significant rescue campaign was possible unless havens were opened. Once America took the step, the other United Nations would undoubtedly follow. Furthermore, the approaching end of the war and the long transatlantic trip meant few refugees would actually come to the United States. The important thing, it stressed, was to offer to receive them.

Before the proposal could go to the White House, it needed the approval of the secretaries of war, state, and the treasury. Stimson, a restrictionist, had serious doubts. He believed that if refugees entered in this way, heavy pressure later on might induce Congress to alter the immigration laws and let them stay. For a time Morgenthau maintained that FDR should not implement the plan without congressional approval. With time, his staff persuaded him that Roosevelt should use his executive powers to carry it out. Hull barely involved himself with the question. Despite the opposition of some of his aides, in the end, Hull went along with Morgenthau. Their recommendation went to the White House on May 8.

Meanwhile, public support was building behind the plan for emergency camps. Early in April, *New York Post* writer Samuel Grafton, whose column ran in forty newspapers with combined circulations of over four million, launched a campaign for "free ports for refugees fleeing the Hitler terror."

The *New York Post* hammered away on the issue in editorials and news articles. The *New York Herald Tribune*, the *New York Times*, the *Christian Science Monitor*, and numerous other papers soon joined the call. So did the entire Hearst chain, syndicated columnist Dorothy Thompson, several radio commentators, the *New Republic*, the *Nation*, *Commonweal*, and the *Christian Century*. The Jewish press and all important Jewish organizations backed the plan. The Bergsonite Emergency Committee dramatized it in full-page newspaper ads linked to a nationwide petition drive.

Among many others to advocate the free-ports proposal were the Federal Council of Churches, the Church Peace Union, the National Board of the

YWCA, the Catholic Committee for Refugees, the Friends and Unitarian service committees, the President's Advisory Committee on Political Refugees, the AFL, the CIO, and the National Farmers Union.

A mid-April Gallup poll requested by presidential assistant David Niles found 70 percent approval of emergency refugee camps in the United States. On May 11, Pehle showed Roosevelt a book of press clippings generated by the proposal, letters of support, and the Gallup poll. The president was impressed. Pehle told him that he thought it was too late to go through Congress, but Roosevelt said he was reluctant to bring in large numbers of refugees without its consent. Instead, he proposed that if a specific group of 500 to 1,000 refugees needed a haven, he would take them in and explain his action in a message to Congress. Just a few days later, the WRB learned of the crisis in southern Italy with the heavy influx of Yugoslav refugees. Pehle sent a message to the president pointing out: "This emergency situation is, I believe, exactly [what] you had in mind. We can break this bottleneck by immediately bringing to the United States approximately 1,000 refugees from southern Italy."

Morgenthau and Pehle went to see Roosevelt on June 1. FDR was aware of the problem and agreed to bring over 1,000 refugees from Italy. Fort Ontario, a vacant Army camp at Oswego, in northern New York, was chosen as their destination. The next day, at his press conference, the president announced that "we are going to bring over a thousand, that's all, to this country, to go into that camp."

Fort Ontario was the only American free port. Eight months earlier, Sweden had taken in 8,000 Jews from Denmark, though her population and land area were each about one-twentieth that of the United States. Journalist I.F. Stone described the American contribution as "a kind of token payment to decency, a bargain-counter flourish in humanitarianism."

Assessing the WRB's Achievements

By the end of the war, the WRB had played a crucial role in saving approximately 200,000 Jews from the Holocaust. About 15,000 were evacuated from Axis territory (as were more than 20,000 non-Jews). At least 10,000, and probably thousands more, were protected within Axis Europe by WRB-financed underground activities and by the board's steps to safeguard holders of Latin American passports. WRB diplomatic pressures, backed by its program of psychological warfare, were instrumental in seeing the 48,000 Jews in Transnistria moved to safe areas of Rumania. Similar pressures helped end the Hungarian deportations. Ultimately, 120,000 Jews survived in Budapest.

The results of other WRB programs, though they unquestionably contributed to the survival of thousands more, can never be quantified. These actions include the war-crimes warnings and the shipments of thousands of food parcels into concentration camps in the last months of the war.

On the other hand, numerous WRB plans that might have succeeded collapsed because the rest of the government did not provide the cooperation legally required of it by Executive Order 9417. Nor could the board wield the diplomatic influence that was needed; its approaches to foreign governments and international organizations always had to go through the State Department, which was often uncooperative. Moreover, President Roosevelt never moved to strengthen the board. And it was always hobbled by the government's failure to fund it properly.

The shortcomings in the WRB's record must not, however, be allowed to overshadow its achievements. As leaders of the private agencies remarked, its staff acted with "enormous drive and energy" and "a fervent sense of desire to get something accomplished." Their dedication broke America's indifference to the destruction of European Jewry, thereby helping to salvage, in some degree, the nation's conscience.

Notes

1. This chapter was composed by David S. Wyman and Rafael Medoff, based on Prof. Wyman's research. Wyman, the grandson of two Protestant ministers, earned his Ph.D. in history from Harvard University, where he was a Woodrow Wilson Fellow. From 1966 until his retirement in 1991 he taught at the University of Massachusetts, Amherst, where he was the Josiah E. DuBois, Jr., Professor of History and twice served as chairman of the Judaic studies program. Professor Wyman is author of *Paper Walls: America and the Refugee Crisis, 1938–1941*; the best-selling *The Abandonment of the Jews: America and the Holocaust, 1941–1945*; and coauthor (with Rafael Medoff) of *A Race against Death: Peter Bergson, America, and the Holocaust*. He edited *The World Reacts to the Holocaust* and *America and the Holocaust*, a thirteen-volume set of documents that he used in the research for *The Abandonment of the Jews*.

2. David S. Wyman, *The Abandonment of the Jews: America and the Holocaust, 1941–1945* (New York: Pantheon, 1984), 385 n5.

Epilogue

Shortly after the war ended, the War Refugee Board, having fulfilled its designated purpose, was disbanded. During the year to follow, DuBois served on U.S. delegations to talks in Berlin, Moscow, and Tokyo about postwar reconstruction. In May 1946, he concluded his government service, and the DuBois family moved back to New Jersey. There DuBois joined his brother Herb's private law practice in Camden, resuming the quiet life that had been interrupted when he was first called to Washington a decade earlier.

DuBois never regarded himself as a hero. As he settled back into civilian life, he made no effort to publicize what he had done during the Holocaust. Richard Goodwin, who met DuBois in later years, found that "it was like pulling teeth" to get him to talk about his experiences in the 1940s.[1] But what DuBois achieved as a whistleblower and rescue activist was indisputably remarkable. He had been the quintessential little guy, battling forces far more powerful than he, in order to save the lives of innocent people half a world away. "Compassionate, idealistic, and vigorous," as Henry Morgenthau III described him,[2] DuBois would not be deterred, not by anonymous threatening phone calls, not by anti-Semitic State Department and Foreign Office officials who sought to sabotage rescue opportunities, nor by the indifference of a president who, in DuBois's words, was "first a politician, and then a humanitarian."[3] DuBois persevered—and triumphed.

As it turned out, he was not quite done.

Josiah and Dorothy DuBois, with their children Robert (standing) and Jeri. Date unknown.

One brisk day in early December 1946, DuBois received an unexpected telephone call. The government wanted him back, this time to head the prosecution in one of the Nuremberg Trials: the case of twenty-four directors of I.G. Farben, the German chemical manufacturing conglomerate. They were to be tried for encouraging German military aggression in order to profit from the conquest of other nations and for their role in the Holocaust by using hundreds of thousands of Jewish slave laborers in their factories and supplying the Nazis with Zyklon B, the poison gas used in the gas chambers at the death camps. In his work for the Treasury Department's Foreign Funds Control Division combating German economic penetration of Latin America, DuBois had repeatedly encountered I.G. Farben's efforts to dominate local industries. "Guatemala was practically a Farben subsidiary," he later wrote.[4]

Coincidentally, the government official who interviewed DuBois and helped convince him to take on the Nuremberg assignment was himself destined to become a hero to the Jewish people. A year after his December 1946 meeting with DuBois, Colonel David "Mickey" Marcus would leave his position as chief of the War Department's War Crimes Division in order to become the first major general of a Jewish army in two thousand years. His leadership is widely credited with rescuing the newborn State of Israel from the five invading Arab armies in the 1948 Arab–Israeli war.[5]

DuBois arrived in Berlin in January 1947. The man who had helped bring about the rescue of an estimated 200,000 Jews from the Holocaust would now

Josiah and Dorothy DuBois in Paris, 1946.

DuBois, at far left, meeting with fellow-prosecutors in 1946 or 1947, during the Nuremberg Trials. The man in uniform is Col. Telford Taylor (1908–1998), who was Chief Counsel in twelve of the thirteen trials.

confront those who had helped murder the millions he was unable to rescue. Over the course of nearly a year, DuBois and his team of prosecutors presented a strong, in some respects overwhelming, case against the accused. Their arguments were bolstered by the defendants' contradictory and often implausible testimony on the witness stand. But when the final verdict was handed down in July 1948, it proved to be a bitter disappointment. Only thirteen of the defendants were convicted on any of the counts; the other ten were acquitted of all charges (the remaining defendant was released because of his health). To make matters worse, the sentences meted out to the guilty were, as DuBois put it, "light enough to please a chicken thief, or a driver who had irresponsibly run down a pedestrian."[6] The I.G. Farben directors received prison terms of from one and a half to eight years, five of them just two years or less.

DuBois was convinced that the verdict and sentencing had been unduly influenced by the prevailing political climate. On the very first day of the trial, one of the three judges had remarked, "We have to worry about the Russians now," a comment DuBois regarded as an omen that the outcome of the proceedings might be shaped by postwar fears of Soviet Communism and the view in some U.S. government circles that Germany needed to be forgiven and embraced so that it would help America stand up to the USSR.[7] During the trial, the Farben directors had justified their admitted role in German militarization by referring to the perceived threat of Communism and, in DuBois's view, the judges were "reading from the current situation" when they refused to hold the Farben directors blameworthy on the charge of encouraging war.[8]

DuBois's analysis of the political environment and its influence on U.S. policy toward Nazi war criminals was soon vindicated by a shift in U.S. policy. In the name of encouraging Germany to help the United States in the Cold War, the

Truman administration retreated from its original plan for a de-Nazification program in postwar Germany that would have included appropriate punishment for all Nazi war criminals. Instead, clemency would become the order of the day. One of the officials who played a key role in this new U.S. policy was John J. McCloy.

Before the war, McCloy (1895–1989) had served as a legal counselor to I.G. Farben. Later, as assistant secretary of war, he was responsible for supervising the relocation and internment of Japanese-Americans, a policy he defended to his dying day, insisting that conditions in the detention camps were "very pleasant." It was McCloy who in 1944 repeatedly rejected requests by the War Refugee Board and Jewish organizations to bomb Auschwitz or the railway lines leading to it. In his letters of rejection, McCloy falsely claimed that the War Department had undertaken a "study" of the bombing issue. He also falsely claimed that bombing the death camp would require a "diversion" of U.S. planes, when, in fact, those planes were already flying over Auschwitz to strike at the I.G. Farben synthetic oil plants, some of which were situated less than five miles from the gas chambers. He went so far as to claim that bombing Auschwitz "might provoke even more vindictive action by the Germans" (McCloy did not explain what could be "more vindictive" than gassing to death 12,000 people each day). Behind the scenes, however, McCloy showed his true colors when he bluntly advised the army's chief of staff that they should not be "getting the Army involved in this [helping the Jews] while the war is on."[9]

McCloy, who had blocked the War Refugee Board's requests to interrupt the mass murder by bombing Auschwitz, would now set free Nazi war criminals who helped carry out that mass murder. Appointed U.S. high commissioner for Germany in 1949, McCloy proceeded to grant clemency to numerous German industrialists convicted of war crimes. One hundred and four German industrial leaders had been found guilty, and eighty-four of them were still in prison at the time McCloy stepped in. Of those eighty-four, McCloy reduced the sentences of seventy-four to time already served, thus granting them immediate freedom. Of the thirteen I.G. Farben directors whom DuBois had put behind bars, eight had already completed their meager sentences; McCloy freed the remaining five.[10] The McCloy pardons provided a cruel and ironic postscript to the DuBois story.

DuBois, however, was not prepared to let McCloy and his ilk have the final word. Leaving the courtroom at Nuremberg after the sentencing of the Farben criminals, DuBois had remarked to a colleague, "I'll write a book about this if it's the last thing I ever do."[11] And so he raised his voice in protest one last time, in a blistering 374-page account of the trial titled *The Devil's Chemists*. Published in 1952, DuBois's book was not merely a scathing portrait of the "generals in gray suits" and the judges who showed them undeserved mercy. It was also a stirring cri de coeur about the broader implications of American policy toward totalitarian regimes. The U.S. strategy of pardoning ex-Nazis in Europe, propping up juntas in Latin America, and supporting dictators in Asia, all in the name of building a "bulwark against Communism," was both morally wrong and doomed to failure, DuBois contended. Forcing smaller countries to "choose between Communism and reliving the dark era of World War II" was likely to drive at least some of them into the arms of the Communists.[12] DuBois could not have imagined the extremes to which this soft-on-Nazis policy could lead. Congressional investigations in the 1970s, followed by legislation requiring the declassification of documents by the CIA and other government agencies, brought these practices to light and revealed that in the aftermath of World War II the U.S. government pardoned, sheltered, and hired numerous Nazi war criminals for various Cold War purposes.[13]

Josiah DuBois in the 1970s.

In Washington, in Nuremberg, and in the pages of *The Devil's Chemists*, Josiah DuBois was a powerful and courageous voice for justice, which some resented but none could stifle. The Breckinridge Longs and John McCloys whom he encountered sometimes managed to frustrate his good work, but those setbacks in no way diminish the greatness of DuBois nor the significance of what he achieved. His heroism will shine forever as a beacon of light in history's darkest era.

NOTES

1. From remarks made by Mr. Goodwin at "Blowing the Whistle on Genocide: Josiah E. DuBois, Jr., and the Struggle for a U.S. Response to the Holocaust," at the University of Pennsylvania School of Law, 11 June 2006 (hereafter Wyman Conference).

2. From remarks made by Mr. Morgenthau at the Wyman conference.

3. Goodwin, Wyman Conference.

4. Josiah E. DuBois, Jr., *The Devil's Chemists* (Boston: The Beacon Press, 1952), 15.

5. DuBois recounts his interview with Marcus in *The Devil's Chemists*, 19–22.

6. *The Devil's Chemists*, 339.

7. Ibid., 338.

8. Ibid.

9. Steve Whitfield, "The Real (John J.) McCloy?" *Moment* 8, no. 8 (September 1983), 45–52.

10. Ibid.

11   DuBois, op. cit., 346.

12.   Op. cit., 363.

13.   For background on U.S. policy toward Nazi war criminals, see Christopher Simpson, *Blowback: America's Recruitment of Nazis and Its Effects on the Cold War* (New York: Weidenfeld & Nicolson, 1988), and Tom Bower, *The Paperclip Conspiracy: The Hunt for the Nazi Scientists* (Boston: Little, Brown, 1988).

Executive Order 9417[1]
Establishing a War Refugee Board

Whereas it is the policy of this Government to take all measures within its power to rescue the victims of enemy oppression who are in imminent danger of death and otherwise to afford such victims all possible relief and assistance consistent with the successful prosecution of the war;

Now, therefore, by virtue of the authority vested in me by the Constitution of the United States and as Commander in Chief of the Army and Navy, and in order to effectuate with all possible speed the rescue and relief of such victims of enemy oppression, it is hereby ordered as follows:

1. There is established in the Executive Office of the President a War Refugee Board (hereinafter referred to as the Board). The Board shall consist of the Secretary of State, the Secretary of the Treasury and the Secretary of War. The Board may request the heads of other agencies or departments to participate in its deliberations whenever matters specially affecting such agencies or departments under consideration.

2. The Board shall be charged with the responsibility for seeing that the policy of the Government, as stated in the Preamble, is carried out. The functions of the Board shall include without limitation the development of plans and programs and the inauguration of effective measures for (a) the rescue, transportation, maintenance and relief of the victims of enemy oppression, and (b) the establishment of havens of temporary refuge for such victims. To this end the Board, through appropriate channels, shall take the necessary steps to enlist the cooperation of foreign governments and obtain their participation in the execution of such plans and programs.

3. It shall be the duty of the State, Treasury and War Departments, within their respective spheres, to execute at the request of the Board, the plans and programs so developed and the measures so inaugurated. It shall be the duty of the heads of all agencies and departments to supply or obtain for the Board such information and to extend to the Board such supplies, shipping and other specified assistance and facilities as the Board may require in carrying out the provisions of this Order. The State Department shall appoint special attachés with diplomatic status, on the recommendation of the Board, to be stationed abroad

in places where it is likely that assistance can be rendered to war refugees, the duties and responsibilities of such attachés to be defined by the Board in consultation with the State Department.

4. The Board and the State, Treasury and War Departments are authorized to accept the services or contributions of any private persons, private organizations, State agencies, or agencies of foreign governments in carrying out the purposes of this Order. The Board shall cooperate with all existing and future international organizations concerned with the problems of refugee rescue, maintenance, transportation, relief, rehabilitation, and resettlement.

5. To the extent possible the Board shall utilize the personnel, supplies, facilities and services of the State, Treasury, and War Departments. In addition the Board, within the limits of funds which may be made available, may employ necessary personnel without regard for the Civil Service laws and regulations and the Classification Act of 1923, as amended, and make provisions for supplies, facilities and services necessary to discharge its responsibilities. The Board shall appoint an Executive Director who shall serve as its principal executive officer. It shall be the duty of the Executive Director to arrange for the prompt execution of the plans and programs developed and the measures inaugurated by the Board, to supervise the activities of the special attachés and to submit frequent reports to the Board on the steps taken for the rescue and relief of war refugees.

6. The Board shall be directly responsible to the President in carrying out the policy of this Government, as stated in the Preamble, and the Board shall report to him at frequent intervals concerning the steps taken for the rescue and relief of war refugees and shall make such recommendations as the Board may deem appropriate for further action to overcome any difficulties encountered in the rescue and relief of war refugees.

Franklin D. Roosevelt
The White House,
Jan. 22, 1944

Note

1.   Federal Register, vol. 9, 26 January 1944, 935–936.

Declaration by the President of the United States

One of the blackest crimes in history, the systematic murder of the Jews of Europe, continues unabated.

The Nazi leaders have made it clear that they have not abandoned the plan to exterminate all the Jews within their grasp. More than two million men, women and children already have been put to death solely because they were Jews.

The world will not forget the Japanese torture of our soldiers nor the slaughters of Lidice, Kharkov and Nanking. The world will not forget the murder of the Jews.

Our youth is fighting and dying on the battlefronts to make a world in which tyranny and barbarity can not exist; a world based upon freedom, equality, and justice; a world in which all persons regardless of race, color or creed may live in peace, honor and dignity.

It is, therefore, fitting that we should again proclaim our determination that none who participate in such acts of savagery shall go unpunished. The United Nations have made it clear that they will pursue the guilty and deliver them up in order that justice be done. Let that warning now be repeated so that no one shall fail to hear and understand. Let it be clearly understood that this applies not only to the leaders but also to their functionaries and subordinates, whether they be in Germany or in the satellite countries. All who knowingly take part in the deportation of Jews to their death in Poland are equally guilty with the executioner. All who share the guilt shall share the punishment.

The Hitlerite forces are committing these crimes against humanity in the name of the German people. Let every German and every man everywhere under Nazi domination by his actions demonstrate to the world that in his heart he does not share these insane desires. Let him hide these victims, help them to get over the borders, and do what he can to save them from the Nazi hangman. Let him also keep watch, and record the evidence that can one day soon be used to convict the guilty and acquit the innocent.

In the meantime, and until the victory that is now assured is won, we shall persevere in our efforts to rescue the victims of Hitler's brutality. In so far as the necessities of military occupations permit, this Government will use all means at its command to aid the escape of Jews and other intended victims of the Nazi executioner. We call upon all the peoples of Europe to lend assistance to this task. We call upon the free peoples of Europe to open their frontiers to the victims of oppression. We shall find havens of refuge for them, and we shall find the means to assure their maintenance and support until the tyrant is driven from their homelands.

In the name of justice and humanity let all freedom loving nations rally to these righteous undertaking.

(Source: "Declaration by the President of the United States," undated [March 1944], Folder 62, Box 3, PSGP.)

The edited version that was used:
IMMEDIATE RELEASE   March 24, 1944

Statement by the President

The United Nations are fighting to make a world in which tyranny and aggression can not exist; a world based upon freedom, equality and justice; a world in which all persons regardless of race, color or creed may live in peace, honor and dignity.

In the meantime in most of Europe and in parts of Asia the systematic torture and murder of civilians—men, women and children—by the Nazis and the Japanese continue unabated. In areas subjugated by the aggressors innocent Poles, Czechs, Norwegians, Dutch, Danes, French, Greeks, Russians, Chinese, Filipinos—and many others—are being starved or frozen to death or murdered in cold blood in a campaign of savagery.

The slaughters of Warsaw, Lidice, Kharkov and Nanking—the brutal torture and murder by the Japanese, not only of civilians but of our own gallant American soldiers and fliers—these are startling examples of what goes on day by day, year in and year out, wherever the Nazis and the Japs are in military control—free to follow their barbaric purposes.

In one of the blackest crimes of all history—begun by the Nazis in the day of peace and multiplied by them a hundred times in time of war—the wholesale systematic murder of the Jews of Europe goes unabated every hour. As a result of the events of the last few days hundreds of thousands of Jews, who while living under persecution have at least found a haven from death in Hungary and the Balkans, are now threatened with annihilation as Hitler's forces descend more heavily upon these lands. That these innocent people, who have already survived a decade of Hitler's fury, should perish on the very eve of triumph over the barbarism which their persecution symbolizes, would be a major tragedy.

It is therefore fitting that we should again proclaim our determination that none who participate in these acts of savagery shall go unpunished. The United

Nations have made it clear that they will pursue the guilty and deliver them up in order that Justice be done. That warning applies not only to the leaders but also their functionaries and subordinates in Germany and in the satellite countries. All who knowingly take part in the deportation of Jews to their death in Poland or Norwegians and French to their death in Germany are equally guilty with the executioner. All who share the guilt shall share the punishment.

Hitler is committing these crimes against humanity in the name of the German people. I ask every German and every man everywhere under Nazi domination to show the world by his action that in his heart he does not share these insane desires. Let him hide these pursued victims, help them to get over their borders, and do what he can to save them from the Nazi hangman. I ask him also to keep watch, and record the evidence that will one day soon be used to convict the guilty.

In the meantime, and until the victory that is now assured is won, we shall persevere in its efforts to rescue the victims of brutality of the Nazis and the Japs. In so far as the necessity of military operations permit this Government will use all means at its command to aid the escape of all intended victims of the Nazi executioner—regardless of race or religion or color. We call upon the free peoples of Europe and Asia temporarily to open their frontiers to all victims of oppression. We shall find havens of refuge for them, and we shall find the means for their maintenance and support until the tyrant is driven from their homelands and they may return.

In the name of justice and humanity let all freedom loving nations rally to these righteous undertaking.

(Source: "Statement by President Roosevelt," 24 March 1944, 740.00116 European War 1939/1368, Records of the State Department, National Archives.)

Leaflet to be Dropped over Germany

Leaflet to be dropped over Germany, as drafted by the War Refugee Board in September 1944:

GERMANS!

There are within your midst large numbers of persons forced-labor battalions and in concentration camps. Without regard to their nationality and whether they are Jewish or otherwise, Germans, these are my orders: You shall disregard any order from whatever source, to molest, or otherwise harm or persecute any of these people. As the Allied armies, already firmly on German soil, advance, we shall expect to find these persons alive and unharmed. Severe penalties will be inflicted upon anyone who is responsible, directly or indirectly, in large measure or in small, for their mistreatment. Those now exercising authority, take heed!
(Source: "Statement by General Eisenhower," undated [27 September 1944], Box 72, War Refugee Board Papers, FDRL.)

The edited version that was used, in November 1944:

Germans! You have in your midst a great many men in concentration camps and forced-labor battalions.

Germans! Do not obey any orders, regardless of their source, urging you to molest, harm or persecute them, no matter what their religion or nationality may be.
The Allies, whose armies have already established a firm foot-hold in Germany, expect, on their advance, to find these people alive and unharmed. Heavy punishment awaits those who, directly or indirectly, and to whatever extent, bear any responsibility for the mistreatment of these people.
May this serve as a warning to whoever at present has the power to issue orders.
(Source: Pehle to Morgenthau, 8 November 1944, MD 791, 103–104)

The State Department Changes Its Position on Nazi War Crimes

"Grew Widens Area of Nazi War Crimes"

By Bertram D. Hulen

(Reprinted from the *New York Times*, 2 February 1945, p. 6.)

Washington, Feb. 1—Germans responsible for crimes within the Reich, including those against Jews and others, beyond any question will be punished, Joseph C. Grew, acting Secretary of State, announced today.

In a statement defining the American position on the question, Mr. Grew said this Government has made "forthright and far-reaching" proposals to the Allies for ways of carrying out this intention. While he would not disclose details to keep the information from the enemy, he said it was clear that the American people want the guilty to be punished and he emphasized that "the Department of State and the Government share that inexorable determination."

Final decision as to procedures will be reached in consultation with the United Nations, fifteen of which are represented on the War Crimes Commission in London.

Mr. Grew referred in his statement to the Moscow Declaration and re-peated statements by President Roosevelt concerning the intention to punish the guilty and then said:

"Over the past months, officers of the Department of State, in consulta-tion with other departments, have worked out proposals as forthright and far-reaching as the objectives announced by the President, which they are intended to implement. They provide for the punishment of German leaders and their associates for their responsibility for the whole broad criminal enterprise devised and executed with ruthless disregard of the very foundations of law and moral-ity, including offenses wherever committed against the rules of war and against minority elements, Jewish and other groups, and individuals."

The statement was regarded as placing the United States and Great Brit-ain in alignment concerning the punishment of those guilty of war crimes and crimes committed against minority groups and individuals by the Germans within the Reich.

Thus the situation appeared to be advancing beyond the state of the War Crimes Commission in London which has been cataloging and listing crimes and also submitting recommendations to the governments.

That commission has recommended punishment of the guilty persons and classing all as war criminals, whether the crimes were committed against Germans within the Reich or against persons in other countries. In view of the statement today, some observers were inclined to believe that the question of classification was becoming subordinate.

Sir Cecil Hurst, the British member, resigned from the War Crimes Commission in the dispute over that question and subsequently it was announced that Herbert C. Pell, the American member, would not return to the commission. He and Sir Cecil had stood stanchly [sic] for punishment of all, and as war criminals.

It was stated today in high quarters, however, that the decision for Mr. Pell not to return was based exclusively in the failure of Congress to make an appropriation for him and in no other consideration. The failure to appropriate was said to have been due to a misunderstanding in Congress with the result that the State Department has requested a special appropriation for the purpose.

While the American and British Governments now appear to be in substantial agreement, at least on the broad lines of punishing the guilty, the attitude of the Russians has not recently been made clear in information received through official channels.

It was noted in this connection that Mr. Grew in his statement quoted President Roosevelt not only as stating, on Aug. 21, 1942, that those charged with crimes would "have to stand in courts of law," but also as saying on Oct. 7, 1942, that the Governments did not intend to "resort to mass reprisals."

Selected Bibliography

Allied Government Responses to the Holocaust

Abella, Irving and Harold Troper. *None Is Too Many: Canada and the Jews of Europe, 1933–1948.* New York: Random House, 1982.

Abzug, Robert H. *America Views the Holocaust, 1933–1945: A Brief Documentary History.* Boston and New York: Bedford/St. Martin's, 1999.

Bartrop, Paul. *Australia and the Holocaust, 1933–1945.* Melbourne: Australian Scholarly Publications, 1993.

Bauer, Yehuda. *Jews for Sale? Nazi-Jewish Negotiations, 1933–1945.* New Haven and London: Yale University Press, 1994.

Breitman, Richard. *Official Secrets: What the Nazis Planned, What the British and America Knew.* New York: Hill and Wang, 1998.

Breitman, Richard and Alan M. Kraut. *American Refugee Policy and European Jewry, 1933–1945.* Bloomington and Indianapolis: Indiana University Press, 1987.

Ephraim, Frank. *Escape to Manila: From Nazi Tyranny to Japanese Terror.* Urbana and Chicago: University of Illinois Press, 2003.

Feingold, Henry L. *Bearing Witness: How America and Its Jews Responded to the Holocaust.* Syracuse, NY: Syracuse University Press, 1995.

Feingold, Henry L. *The Politics of Rescue: The Roosevelt Administration and the Holocaust, 1938–1945.* New Brunswick, NJ: Rutgers University Press, 1970.

Friedman, Saul S. *No Haven for the Oppressed: United States Policy toward Refugees, 1938–1945.* Detroit: Wayne State University Press, 1973.

Fry, Varian. *Surrender on Demand.* Boulder, CO: Johnson Books, 1997.

Genizi, Haim. *American Apathy: The Plight of Christian Refugees from Nazism.* Ramat Gan, Israel: Bar-Ilan University Press, 1983.

Gilbert, Martin. *Auschwitz and the Allies.* New York: Holt Rinehart and Winston, 1981.

Hirschmann, Ira A. *Life Line to a Promised Land.* New York: Vanguard Press, 1946.

Jackman, Jarrell C. and Carla M. Borden. *The Muses Flee Hitler: Cultural Transfer and Adaptation, 1930–1945.* Washington, D.C.: Smithsonian Institution Press, 1983.

Laqueur, Walter. *The Terrible Secret.* Boston and Toronto: Little Brown, 1980.

Laqueur, Walter and Richard Breitman. *Breaking the Silence.* New York: Simon and Schuster, 1986.

Lowenstein, Sharon R. *Token Refuge: The Story of the Jewish Refugee Shelter in Oswego, 1944–1946.* Bloomington: Indiana University Press, 1986.

Marino, Andy. *A Quiet American: The Secret War of Varian Fry.* New York: St. Martin's Press, 1999.

Morse, Arthur D. *While Six Million Died: A Chronicle of American Apathy.* New York: Random House, 1967.

Penkower, Monty Noam. *The Holocaust and Israel Reborn: From Catastrophe to Sovereignty.* Urbana and Chicago: University of Illinois Press, 1994.

Penkower, Monty Noam. *The Jews Were Expendable: Free World Diplomacy and the Holocaust.* Urbana and Chicago: University of Illinois Press, 1983.

Perl, William R. *The Four-Front War: From the Holocaust to the Promised Land.* New York: Crown, 1978.

Smith, Sharon Kay. "Elbert D. Thomas and America's Response to the Holocaust." Ph.D. dissertation, Brigham Young University, 1992.

Thomas, Gordon and Max Morgan Witts. *Voyage of the Damned.* New York: Stein and Day, 1974.

Vrba, Rudolf and Alan Bestic. *I Cannot Forgive.* New York: Grove Press, 1964.

Wasserstein, Bernard. *Britain and the Jews of Europe, 1939–1945.* New York and Oxford: Oxford University Press, 1979.

Weisberg, Alex. *Desperate Mission.* New York: Criterion Books, 1958.

Wood, E. Thomas and Stanislaw M Jankowski. *Karski: How One Man Tried to Stop the Holocaust.* New York: John Wiley and Sons, 1994.

Wyman, David S. *The Abandonment of the Jews: America and the Holocaust, 1941–1945.* New York: Pantheon, 1984.

Wyman, David S. *America and the Holocaust.* 13 vols. New York: Garland, 1993.

Wyman, David S. *Paper Walls: America and the Refugee Crisis, 1938–1941.* Amherst: University of Massachusetts Press, 1968.

Wyman David S., ed. *The World Reacts to the Holocaust.* Baltimore: Johns Hopkins University Press, 1996.

Zucker, Bat-Ami. *In Search of Refuge: Jews and U.S. Consuls in Nazi Germany, 1933–1941.* London and Portland, ME: Vallentine Mitchell, 2001.

American Media Coverage of the Holocaust

Leff, Laurel. *Buried by the* Times: *The Holocaust and America's Most Important Newspaper.* New York: Cambridge University Press, 2005.

Lipstadt, Deborah E. *Beyond Belief: The American Press and the Coming of the Holocaust, 1933–1945.* New York: The New Press, 1986.

Shapiro, Robert Moses, ed. *Why Didn't the Press Shout? American and International Journalism During the Holocaust.* New York: Yeshiva University Press, 2003.

American Christian Responses

Ross, Robert W. *So It Was True: The American Protestant Press and the Nazi Persecution of the Jews.* Minneapolis: University of Minnesota Press, 1980.

American Jewish Responses

Arad, Gulie Ne'eman. *America, Its Jews, and the Rise of Nazism.* Bloomington and Indianapolis: Indiana University Press, 2000.

Bauer, Yehuda. *American Jewry and the Holocaust: The American Jewish Joint Distribution Committee, 1939–1945.* Detroit: Wayne State University Press, 1981.

Bauer, Yehuda. *My Brother's Keeper: A History of the American Jewish Joint Distribution Committee, 1929–1939.* Philadelphia: Jewish Publication Society of America, 1974.

Baumel, Judith Tydor. *The "Bergson Boys" and the Origins of Contemporary Militancy.* Syracuse, NY: Syracuse University Press, 2005.

Ben-Ami, Yitshaq. *Years of Wrath, Days of Glory: Memoirs from the Irgun.* New York: Shengold, 1983.

Berman, Aaron. *Nazism, the Jews, and American Zionism.* Detroit: Wayne State University Press, 1990.

Gottlieb, Moshe. "The Anti-Nazi Boycott Movement in the American Jewish Community, 1933–1941." Ph.D. dissertation, Brandeis University, 1967.

Grobman, Alex. *Battling for Souls: The Vaad Hatzala Rescue Committee in Post-War Europe.* Jersey City, NJ: Ktav, 2003.

Hecht, Ben. *A Child of the Century.* New York: Simon & Schuster, 1954.

Korff, Baruch. *Flight from Fear.* New York: Elmar, 1953.

Lookstein, Haskel. *Were We Our Brothers' Keepers? The Public Response of American Jews to the Holocaust, 1938–1944.* New York: Hartmore House, 1985.

Medoff, Rafael. *The Deafening Silence: American Jewish Leaders and the Holocaust.* New York: Steimatzky-Shapolsky, 1987.

Medoff, Rafael. *Militant Zionism in America: The Rise and Impact of the Jabotinsky Movement in the United States, 1926–1948.* Tuscaloosa: University of Alabama Press, 2002.

Neuringer, Sheldon Morris. "American Jewry and United States Immigration Policy, 1881–1953." Ph.D. dissertation, University of Wisconsin, 1969.

Neustadt-Noy, Isaac. "The Unending Task: Efforts to Unite American Jewry from the American Jewish Congress to the American Jewish Conference." Ph.D. dissertation, Brandeis University, 1976.

Nurenberger, M.J. *The Scared and the Doomed: The Jewish Establishment vs. the Six Million.* Ontario: Mosaic Press, 1985.

Rafaeli, Alex. *Dream and Action: The Story of My Life.* Jerusalem: Achva, 1993.

Rapoport, Louis. *Shake Heaven and Earth: Peter Bergson and the Struggle to Rescue the Jews of Europe.* Jerusalem: Gefen, 1999.

Wolk, Kenneth. "New Haven and Waterbury, Connecticut Jewish Communities' Public Response to the Holocaust, 1938–1944." Ph.D. dissertation, New York University, 1995.

Wyman, David S. and Rafael Medoff. *A Race against Death: Peter Bergson, America, and the Holocaust.* New York: The New Press, 2002.

Zuroff, Efraim. *The Response of Orthodox Jewry in the United States to the Holocaust: The Activities of the Vaad-ha-Hatzala Rescue Committee, 1939–1945.* New York: Yeshiva University Press, 2000.

Index

About the Author

Dr. Rafael Medoff is founding director of The David S. Wyman Institute for Holocaust Studies (www.WymanInstitute.org), which focuses on issues related to America's response to the Holocaust. Dr. Medoff is the author of seven books about the Holocaust, Zionism, and the history of American Jewry, including, most recently, *A Race against Death: Peter Bergson, America, and the Holocaust* (coauthored with David S. Wyman). His textbook *Jewish Americans and Political Participation* was named an Outstanding Academic Title of 2003 by the American Library Association's *Choice* magazine.

He has taught Jewish history at Ohio State University, Purchase College of the State University of New York, and elsewhere and served as associate editor of the scholarly journal *American Jewish History*. His essays have appeared in numerous academic journals, and he has authored entries for many reference volumes, including *American National Biography* and the *Encyclopedia Judaica*.